HELLO

MY NAME IS

Few people are making jokes about the Church these days. Most Christians are dead serious about their churches. Where they are growing, people are excited and anxious to do their part to keep things moving for the glory of God. Where they are declining, people want to know the reasons why and what they can do about it.

Finding the answers to the question of why churches are growing or not growing is what the Church Growth Movement is all about. There are many different ways of approaching the task of discovering what God is doing in today's world. And one of them is to look around the country at the churches that seem to be doing something unusual and, consequently, are maintaining a steady pattern of growth.

Just what is it that makes churches like these grow? Of course, it is, in the final analysis, God at work through His Holy Spirit. But if we study these churches and others like them more closely, we can learn more about the way God works.

And that is what this book is all about.

—C.P.W.

OTHER BOOKS BY THE SAME AUTHOR

The Condor of the Jungle (with Joseph S. Mc-Cullough; Fleming H. Revell Co.)

Defeat of the Bird God (William Carey Library)

Latin American Theology (Wm. B. Eerdmans Publishing Co.)

The Protestant Movement in Bolivia (William Carey Library)

An Extension Seminary Primer (with Ralph Covell; William Carey Library)

A Turned-on Church in an Uptight World (Zondervan Publishing House)

Frontiers in Missionary Strategy (Moody Press)

Church/Mission Tensions Today (editor; Moody Press)

Look Out! The Pentecostals Are Coming (Creation House)

Stop the World I Want to Get On (Regal Books)

your church can GROW

BY C. PETER WAGNER

Study Questions by Rev. John Wimber

A Division of G/L Publications
Glendale, California, U.S.A.

Dedicated
to
Ray Ortlund,
the pastoral staff,
and my Christian brothers and sisters
in Lake Avenue Congregational Church
Pasadena, California

Scripture quotations, as indicated, are from:
The King James Version
The Living Bible, Paraphrased. (Taylor) Wheaton: Tyndale House,
Publishers, 1971. Used by permission.
The Revised Standard Version, copyrighted 1946 and 1952 by the
Division of Christian Education of the NCCC in the U.S.A. and
used by permission.

Published by

Regal Books Division, G/L Publications
Glendale, California 91209, U.S.A.

Library of Congress Catalog Card No. 75-39410
ISBN 0-8307-0414-0

contents

foreword

I want you to know my friend Peter Wagner. There is no one else like him.

Several years ago Sunday evening service was in progress at Lake Avenue Congregational Church, and we were receiving new members. They were lined up across the front of the church and I asked if any would like to tell us how they came to know Jesus Christ.

One by one, dear people gave testimony of the blessing of receiving the Lord. Then a puckish man stepped forward. He had a graying goatee and twinkling eyes, and with a sneaky, disarming sort of charisma, he began, "Well, when I was a young man on the farm, one day I was milking a cow. A beautiful girl whom I had never seen before walked into the barn. It was love at first sight, so I squirted some milk on her toe . . . The next thing I knew she was inviting me to church, and a few months later she led me to the Lord. . . ."

Amid roars of laughter, the personality of Peter Wagner had arrived on the Lake Avenue scene, and none of us has been the same since—or would want to be. Peter has given himself indefatigably to us, preaching and teaching among us as needed, adding his input as a top world authority on church growth, and besides all that, simply loving us and charming us.

This is Peter's eleventh book: his eleventh while being a missionary, then the head of his mission, then a student in the School of World Mission at Fuller Theological Seminary; then a doctoral candidate at the University of Southern California, a professor at the School of World Mission and Director of the Fuller Evangelistic Association as well as a preacher, conference speaker and world strategist. And all that on top of being a husband to his wonderful partner Doris, and the father of Karen, Ruth and Rebecca.

Now you must read this book on American church growth. Pastors and lay people alike need to look hard at the scientific measurements of a church and what makes it grow or not grow. And they need also simply to get stars in their eyes as God renews their vision of winning the lost around them to Christ.

And reading a book like this one is not hard, because Peter loves life, loves the Lord with all his heart, and loves the church and his writing shows it. His innovative way of thinking will challenge you and I hope move you. Peter is out on the growing edge of life—out there with God, and going ahead with Him.

I'm glad I know him.

—Raymond C. Ortlund

acknowledgments

First of all, I wish to acknowledge, as a member, my debt to the Lake Avenue Congregational Church of Pasadena, California and to Pastor Ray Ortlund for the leadership he has given that church. Since I will be making frequent reference to Lake Avenue Church throughout this book—after all, it is the church I know best—it is appropriate that I identify my personal commitment from the outset.

I sense a responsibility as a church growth specialist to combine broad exposure to a large number of churches around the world with a deep involvement in the one church where I have my membership. I would feel strange to advocate that the proper goal of evangelism is to bring people into responsible church membership if I were not an active and responsible church member myself.

I am not reticent to admit that I love my church. I can only hope that all who read this book love their churches as much or more. If so, all will understand any bias that might show through in what I hope will otherwise be as objective a presentation as possible.

Also, I am grateful to several Christian leaders who read portions of the manuscript and offered their encouragement and suggestions. They include Donald McGavran, Win Arn, John Wimber, Paul Benjamin, Dennis Oliver, Harold Lindsell, Elmer Towns, Jack Hyles, Raymond Ortlund, Robert Schuller, Wilbert Eichenberger, David Libby, Daniel Baumann, James Conklin, Albert Runge, Donald Hamman, Phillip Goble, David Mains and undoubtedly others to whom I will later apologize for not recalling their names at the moment.

Finally, after 25 short years of marriage, I feel more than ever before that this book is a team effort. The advantages of being married to a woman who at once is an efficient full-time private secretary and a Betty Crocker quality homemaker are beyond my powers of description. I can only give praise to God for Doris, whose keen critical eye combined with professional typing skills has given the manuscript whatever polish and precision it can claim.

C. Peter Wagner

where did church growth come from?

"Evangelicals from all points on the ecclesiological continuum agree: the Church Growth Movement is 'hot,' the debate it has stirred is getting hotter, and evangelicals around the world—not just those in the U.S.—are going to have to deal with it."

With these words, Robert Coote of *Eternity* magazine introduces a special report on what he considers to be "one of the most stimulating, yet controversial developments in today's church."

This is a book about that "hot" movement. It is one of the first systematic attempts to apply the scientific principles of church growth as developed by Donald McGavran specifically to the American scene. In one sense it is overdue. In fact the impact of the whole Church Growth Movement on America is overdue.

The movement itself is 20 years old, but only within the last year or two have Christians in America become aware that there is such a thing as a well-established field of church growth. Since most of us are conditioned—rather ethnocentrically—to "hot" ideas being generated in the U.S. and then exported abroad, this reversal comes as a surprise. Church growth has been conceived as applying chiefly to the church as it expanded on new ground in the Third World; only recently has it been applied to America.

It would be a mistake to imagine that only evangelicals are taking an interest in church growth philosophy as a helpful and creative way of analyzing American religion. Many of the mainline churches as well are asking for accurate insights as to why some churches grow and why some decline. Perhaps the first to take an official action on the matter was the United Presbyterian Church.

In the 1975 General Assembly a working Committee on Church Growth was established to help relate United Presbyterians to the movement. One of the committee's preliminary recommendations was that the denominational seminaries begin to offer courses on local church growth. This is greatly needed because virtually no one in the ministry today ever took a course in church growth in seminary.

Where Church Growth Comes From

Church growth as a movement entered North America in the fall of 1972. It took root in the mind and ministry of Donald McGavran while he was serving as a third-generation missionary to India over a period of 30 years. His first attempts at putting his ideas into writing date back to 1936.

But the widespread diffusion of the movement began with his publication *The Bridges of God* (1955, Friendship Press) and *How Churches Grow* (1959, Friendship Press). These brought church growth, as it applied to *world* evangelization, to national and international attention. The books were extensively reviewed in missionary journals on both sides of the Atlantic and around the world.

How Churches Grow applies also to church growth in America. One of its chapters was reprinted as a booklet under the title *Do Churches Grow?* It sold some thousands of copies among American church leaders, but failed to light any fires. The time was not yet ripe.

11

"Church Growth" Defined

The term "church growth" is a McGavranism. At first Mc-Gavran attempted to phrase the insights he had developed using more traditional language such as "evangelism" or "missions," but he soon found that these terms were little more than useless. They had been defined and redefined so much that they had lost their cutting edge. When "evangelism" and "missions" came to mean everything good that Christians did individually and collectively, they then meant practically nothing.

So in order to describe, in a precise way, what he was trying to articulate, Donald McGavran took two common words and welded them together. Now "church growth" as a technical phrase is as independent from "church" and "growth" as "Grape Nuts" is from "grapes" and "nuts." Actually "church growth" means *all that is involved in bringing men and women who do not have a personal relationship to Jesus Christ into fellowship with Him and into responsible church membership.*

The Institute of Church Growth

After the publication of *The Bridges of God* and *How Churches Grow,* McGavran found himself in high demand as a speaker and seminar leader. Soon he realized, however, that such an itinerant ministry would exert only a minimal influence on the world of missions. So he decided to found a new institution designed to bring together career missionaries on furlough who could master church growth principles on a graduate level, field test them, and transfer the concepts to others.

The "Institute of Church Growth" grew out of that vision, and Northwest Christian College in Eugene, Oregon, offered both sponsorship and hospitality. McGavran's own background in the Christian Church made the association a natural, and classes began there in 1961.

The Move to Fuller Seminary

It wasn't long, however, until the Institute outgrew its first home. In 1965 it moved to Fuller Theological Seminary in Pasadena,

California, where it became the School of World Mission and Institute of Church Growth.

After coming to Fuller, McGavran recruited his first faculty colleague, Australian Alan Tippett. Tippett had developed concepts similar to McGavran's over a twenty-year missionary career in the Fiji Islands, had been a Research Fellow of McGavran's in Eugene and had been an instructor in the Institute of Church Growth.

The faculty has since been strengthened by the addition of four others with missionary experience: Ralph Winter (Guatemala), Arthur Glasser (China), Charles Kraft (Nigeria) and myself (Bolivia). J. Edwin Orr, who teaches part time in the field of the history of awakenings, completes the group at what Robert Coote calls "the Fuller stronghold in Pasadena."

The Objective of Church Growth

Some people do not realize that McGavran developed the theory of church growth and founded his institution with a precisely defined objective: to make more effective the propagation of the gospel and the multiplication of churches *on new ground.* He believed that the expenditure of $300 million a year out of North America for overseas missions could be made to yield much more Christianization. To this end he planned to spread the church growth school of thought among mission executives, career missionaries, and national church leaders working in Asia, Africa and Latin America.

McGavran recognized, of course, that church growth principles apply universally; but he decided to concentrate on the tremendous population overseas. He illustrated his principles almost entirely from missions and new denominations overseas. Consequently the few Christian workers dedicated to ministry in Canada and the United States who attended his classes or seminars or read his books, did not think of church growth as applying to America.

Launching Church Growth in America

Interestingly, when McGavran was teaching missions in the

13

seminaries of the Christian Church in the late 1950s, his students preparing for American ministry frequently said to him, "The principles you teach apply here."

He would reply, "Yes, they do, but how they apply you will have to work out."

In 1963 he planned to add to the Institute of Church Growth at Eugene an American Division headed by an American minister of church growth convictions, but the plan did not mature. In 1967 the annual Church Growth Seminar at Winona Lake, Indiana, drew in about 20 American ministers and heads of Home Missions Departments.

So until 1972, church growth continued to appear chiefly applicable to other lands. A top level American evangelical leader recently said to me, "Somehow I never knew what church growth was. I always thought it was just something out there on the mission field."

He sounded as if he felt he had been slightly cheated. Maybe he had been!

It is more accurate, however, to state that lack of interest in church growth was largely conditioned by defensive thinking. This rationale maintained on many grounds that the true Christian is not interested in mere numbers.

Since many American churches were not growing, church leaders and seminary professors had constructed an extensive defense, partly theological, *against* church growth. This position glorified littleness and "quality" and maintained that growth in numbers is somewhat disreputable. One of McGavran's great contributions is his twenty-year assault on this non-biblical position.

His magnum opus, *Understanding Church Growth* (Eerdmans), was published in 1970. It played a part in preparing America for church growth. It treated church growth on a global basis, vigorously exposed the fallacy of defensive thinking, and stated the universal principles which characterize it. He illustrated growth principles almost entirely from the expansion of churches overseas. It must be considered the *Magna Carta* of the church growth movement.

14

Applying Church Growth to America

The conscious attempt to apply church growth philosophy to America was stimulated in the fall of 1972 by Pastor Charles Miller, then a staff member of Pasadena's Lake Avenue Congregational Church, where I have my membership. At Miller's urging, I organized and asked McGavran to team-teach with me a pilot course in church growth designed specifically for American church leaders.

We did it only as an experiment, but the results were remarkable:

One of the students, Win Arn, left his position with the Evangelical Covenant Church and founded the influential Institute for American Church Growth.

Charles Miller himself resigned his position at Lake Avenue Church and enrolled in the School of World Mission to move deeper into what for him was a fascinating field of study. He now is leading Discipling Ministry Seminars throughout America and is endeavoring to integrate church growth thinking into them.

Phil Goble, another student, used the insights he received in the class to develop a creative model for Jewish evangelism which he more appropriately calls "synagogue growth." Since then he has helped establish one successful Messianic synagogue in Encino, California and is now working on another one on the East Coast. His principles are being widely propagated through his new book, *Everything You Need to Grow a Messianic Synagogue* (1974, William Carey Library).

Promoting Church Growth in America

Apparently, the time was ripe. A few years previously, with all the social turmoil in the U.S.A., American churchmen had not been so receptive to church growth teaching. One of the first advocates of the idea was Wade Coggins of the Evangelical Foreign Missions Association, who wrote in the March, 1967 *United Evangelical Action:* "Up to now, church growth research and training have been aimed toward the missionary front. What about pastors in the U.S.? Should they not be equally interested and equally in need of this philosophy and emphasis? . . . A way must be found to gather the facts on significant growth in this country and disseminate this information to stimulate the church into dynamic growth."

But apparently, few in the turbulent sixties were able to hear what Wade Coggins was saying over the din of the civil rights controversies, the hippie movement and the Viet Nam war.

Two prominent American publishers gave a significant boost to church growth in America during that pivotal year of 1972. The first was William Petersen of *Eternity*, who sent me a collection of books and magazine clippings he had accumulated and asked me for an article on the subject. I wanted to write the article, but I couldn't do it because I simply did not know that much about the American church and how it grows.

It took me almost two years to gain enough understanding of the church in my own native land to fulfill the assignment, but the product of the research was very well received. It was published not only in *Eternity,* but also in *United Evangelical Action* and other places. The National Association of Evangelicals did an offprint under the title "American Church Growth" and has since circulated thousands of that printing.

This book is a further development of the same research project, which now has become a permanent part of my scholarly interests.

Harold Lindsell of *Christianity Today* was the second publisher to nudge church growth theoreticians toward America. "If this is the School of *World* Mission," he once said to a meeting of the faculty, "I want to know if you consider America to be a part of the *world?*"

When the answer was affirmative, he challenged the S.W.M. faculty to apply their insights to the developing nationwide Key 73 evangelistic program, and offered the entire January 19, 1973, issue of *Christianity Today* as a platform. All six faculty members accepted the challenge and contributed essays. But response was minimal, and the effort turned out to be too little too late to rescue Key 73 from evangelistic impotence.

16

Church Growth Pioneers

When the roster of pioneers of church growth in North America is drawn up, three individuals will deserve a prominent place on it:

One is Win C. Arn, one of the students in the first Fuller Seminary course in American Church Growth. In 1973 he and his wife, Barbara, trusted God and stepped out in faith to found the Institute for American Church Growth with headquarters in Arcadia, California. Two excellent films, *How to Grow a Church* and *Reach Out and Grow,* have been produced. Remarkably effective seminar approaches to motivating pastors and lay leadership in local churches have been developed. The Institute publishes a bulletin called *Church Growth: America,* which contains news of Institute activities as well as helpful information for all interested in church growth.

Another pioneer is Paul Benjamin, who in 1974 left his position as Professor of New Testament and Church Growth at Lincoln Christian Seminary to establish the National Church Growth Research Center in Washington, D.C. With access to the Library of Congress, the center is designed to offer outstanding study facilities. Academic work done there is eligible for credit from Lincoln Seminary. Benjamin's paperback, *The Growing Congregation* (1972, Lincoln Christian College Press), is the first direct effort to apply church growth principles to the American context by a denominational publishing house.

The third pioneer is Canadian Dennis Oliver, founder of the Canadian Church Growth Center in Regina, Saskatchewan. Recipient of one of the first Doctor of Missiology degrees from the Fuller School of World Mission, Oliver now teaches on the faculty of the Canadian Theological College. He is responsible for the publication of *Church Growth Canada*—a counterpart to McGavran's *Church Growth Bulletin,* for the Canadian Church Growth Book Club, and for an assortment of seminars and workshops that are spreading church growth philosophy throughout the Canadian provinces.

17

Publishing Church Growth in America

Church Growth Bulletin, the 16-page bimonthly publication edited by Donald McGavran, has been perhaps the chief vehicle for the diffusion of church growth ideas since it was first circulated in 1964. Although half of its 6,000 subscribers are Americans, it is still not well known in the U.S.A.

Yet, because the *Church Growth Bulletin* is read regularly with much profit by missionaries of all stripes, the publication enjoys a far greater influence than its size would suggest. For example, McGavran's hard-hitting article, "Will Uppsala Betray the Two Billion?" made an impact on the leadership of the World Council of Churches that has not yet been forgotten.

Subscribers to the *Church Growth Bulletin* automatically receive membership in the Church Growth Book Club which offers substantial discounts on books dealing with both worldwide and specifically American aspects of church growth.

Several book publishers have recognized the expanding market for church growth information in America. The leader to date has been Regal Books, a division of Gospel Light Publications of Glendale, California. Two of their books are authored by recognized leaders in the field: *God's Way to Keep a Church Going and Growing* by Vergil Gerber of Evangelical Missions Information Service (1973), and *How to Grow a Church,* co-authored by Donald McGavran and Win Arn (1973).

Regal has also published two of the finest case studies of growing churches in America: *Your Church Has Real Possibilities* by Robert Schuller of Garden Grove Community Church (1974) and *Hope for Your Church* by Harold Fickett, formerly of First Baptist Church of Van Nuys (1972).

Although he does not specifically identify with the church growth movement, probably the most prolific writer on growing churches in America is Elmer Towns, who contributes regularly to *Christian Life.* He directs the Sunday School Research Institute of Savannah, Georgia. Much of Towns' writing describes Bible Baptist Fellowship and other fundamentalist churches, among which are some of the fastest growing churches in the nation.

Lyle Schaller has an excellent series of nine books, dealing mostly with mainline denominations. His latest is *Hey, That's Our Church!* (1975, Abingdon).

Church Growth Seminars

For many years the Evangelical Foreign Missions Association sponsored annual church growth seminars, conducted by Donald McGavran and his colleagues, in Winona Lake, Indiana; on the campus of the Alliance School of Missions at Nyack, New York; and on the campus of Biola College in La Mirada, California. Enrollment in these was largely limited to missionary personnel, and the teaching was directed toward cross-cultural ministry in the Third World.

The Biola seminar has now phased out. The Winona Lake seminar was incorporated into the Summer Institute of Missions in the Wheaton College Graduate School in 1972. A two-week session carrying M.A. level credit is held there every summer for both missionaries and U.S. church leaders.

The Nyack seminar has developed a separate section for U.S. pastors, providing an excellent non-academic introduction to church growth principles. The National Association of Evangelicals has also held several series of one-day church growth seminars using speakers such as Pastor Peter Unruh of Wooddale Baptist Church, Minneapolis.

Church Growth for Credit

Academically accredited courses on church growth in seminars and Bible schools are still relatively scarce in North America, but offerings are growing. Until recently, only Fuller Seminary and two institutions affiliated with McGavran's denomination— Lincoln Christian College and Seminary and Milligan College— have offered church growth training.

Other than the program of Fuller's School of World Mission— which requires field missionary experience for enrollment and thus excludes most American pastors—the best graduate training in church growth that I am aware of is the two-week Doctor

19

of Ministry seminar offered every winter by the Fuller School of Theology in Pasadena. The basic responsibility for the seminar is mine, but I am also assisted by Donald McGavran, Win Arn and John Wimber of the Fuller Evangelistic Association.

I anticipate a multiplication of these opportunities for specialized training in church growth in the very near future. I have been invited by Bethel Seminary of St. Paul, Minnesota, for example, to initiate a church growth component of their Doctor of Ministry program.

The major danger I see during this period of development is that some institutions, just to jump on the church growth band-wagon, will list offerings in "church growth" bearing only faint resemblance to the movement I am describing here. One of the early signs of this trend is a brochure I have before me announcing a "Congress on Church Growth." Not one of the speakers is a professional in the field of church growth!

Professional Consultation for Growth

One of the most exciting results of the emerging field of church growth is the creation of a new kind of Christian vocation, that of the professional church growth consultant. A pioneer in this field is Pastor John Wimber of Yorba Linda Friends Church in Orange County, California. Wimber has recently resigned his pastorate to head up the newly-created Department of Church Growth of the Fuller Evangelistic Association. He is now offering his services to churches and denominations much as a physician offers his services to patients.

A successful businessman before his conversion and call to the ministry, Wimber brings a very important credential to church growth: he has been an effective pastor in the U.S.A. The Yorba Linda Friends Church had leveled out at 200 members when he took leadership five years ago. By the time he left, it had grown to 900 and in the meantime he had planted four new Friends churches in the area. Whereas some of us are theoreticians, others like Wimber, are becoming the practitioners of the move-ment.

While taking the Doctor of Ministry seminar at Fuller Seminary, Wimber became convinced that God was calling him to full-time involvement. He had accumulated some previous experience at consultation with good results. He has gifts in the areas of teaching and counseling. The services he has developed under Fuller Evangelistic Association might well provide a model which soon will be reproduced all over the country as God raises up full-time professionals in the field.

The Future of Church Growth

The United States has about 330,000 churches. There are another 20,000 in Canada. Of them, how many are hurting? How many could reverse discouraging patterns of stagnation and decline and begin to grow if they just had the help to do it?

Could there be 50,000? 100,000? If so, we must trust God to multiply the Paul Benjamins, the Win Arns, the John Wimbers, the Dennis Olivers and the Lyle Schallers, for no one has the full answer to all the problems of American churches.

There is no such thing as a panacea for all ills, whether human or church. And church growth itself is a young science, so its contribution as yet is necessarily limited. Progress will require hard work and full dedication, for understanding and analyzing the dynamics of church growth is a complex matter.

I see a new day dawning for the American church. Tremendous human and spiritual powers, now locked into restrictive patterns and outmoded methodologies, will soon be released for the accelerated spread of the Kingdom of God on our continent. If so, all those who love the Lord and are willing to serve Him are in for exciting times!

C. Peter Wagner
Fuller Theological Seminary
Pasadena
January, 1976

to grow or not to grow?

You are enroute to Fort Lauderdale, Florida. But you don't drive for long on North Federal Highway before you see in the distance the 303-foot tower of the Coral Ridge Presbyterian Church. And when you spot it, you have identified the tallest building between the rocket launching pads of Cape Kennedy and the city of Miami.

The $6,000,000 Coral Ridge structure was originally designed to seat 2,500 so that the whole congregation could worship together at 11:00 on Sunday mornings. However, the church had already grown so much between the drawing of the plans and the dedication of the building that two services were needed from the beginning.

Coral Ridge Presbyterian

Many factors are contributing to the growth of Coral Ridge Presbyterian. Not the least of them is a dedicated, gifted, well-trained corps of 450 men and women who move out from the church week after week seeking unsaved people and introducing them to Jesus Christ.

Pastor James Kennedy long ago found that growth in his church had been stifled because the people had the attitude that the pastor should do all the evangelism. He now says, "Letting clerical George do it is the greatest heresy that has plagued the church!"

A film that dramatizes what is going on in Fort Lauderdale is entitled, *Like a Mighty Army*. Spend a week in Fort Lauderdale, and you will see that the army is for real.

Redwood Chapel

Now visit Redwood Chapel in Castro Valley, California near San Francisco. In Fort Lauderdale you found a stately worship service with the ministers in full academic regalia and the ushers all dressed in sky blue tuxedos with black velvet trim. In Castro Valley the only people with specially fancy dress are the musical groups.

Probably few churches in the country have developed the variety of professional-quality small singing groups that you see and hear in Redwood Chapel. The music is so good that church members invite their neighbors to church with no reservation. They know their friends will like it. They would invite even Lawrence Welk if he were in the neighborhood!

Their sanctuary which seats 650 is packed out at each of the two Sunday morning services. When the crowds get too big, large groups of them hive off and start new churches in the area. The new churches develop new musical groups and the new neighbors like it. Many of them are introduced to Jesus Christ and the daughter churches are growing as well as the mother.

First Nazarene, Denver

A mile high in Denver, Colorado, the First Church of the Nazarene has grown from 240 members to 2,000 over the past six years. When Pastor Don Wellman went to Denver six years ago, he had set a goal of building a great church for God. He knew that churches can become involved in lots of good activities, but he and his people were single-minded. He says, "We're only interested in one thing—sharing the claims of the gospel with the world."

The world seems to like the claims of the gospel that First Nazarene presents. In 1974 they moved out of their old building into a 3,800-seat sanctuary. Often 3,000 gather for worship on a Sunday morning.

Pastor Wellman has an eight-point program he is implementing: prayer, youth, music, outreach, education, personal evangelism, senior citizens and Sunday service programs.

First Baptist, Hammond

On Sunday mornings Hammond, Indiana and surrounding communities are virtually crawling with blue buses bearing the motto: "World's Largest Sunday School" across their sides. If you don't know where the church is, you can soon get the directions from one of the 200 bus captains you are bound to meet. Special duty policemen from the Hammond Police Department need to be assigned to the neighborhood of First Baptist Church on Sunday mornings to direct the traffic.

The area where the church is located in downtown Hammond is no suburban country club setting. It is typical inner city: run down, slightly depressed. Many stores and businesses have vacated their buildings, but if it's near the church no sooner does a store get vacated than First Baptist moves in and converts it to Sunday School classrooms.

The First Baptist folk need all the space they can get. One week they had over 30,000 out to Sunday School and they averaged 13,505 during 1974.

New England

On a picturesque seven-acre piece of farmland, Trinity Congregational Church of Bolton, Massachusetts is located in a barn, no less. It is not a big church, but it is a growing, exciting church. When Pastor David Libby started leading his people into discovering their spiritual gifts the church doubled in a year, and now the barn is not large enough for the crowd.

In nearby Vermont, the North Avenue Alliance Church of Burlington has recently become the second largest church in the state. Since Burlington is a university community, special programs have been developed for the university students. On Sunday morning, for example, Yellow Cabs pull up to the church and discharge their passengers without collecting a fare. Any college student who needs transportation to church can call a taxi, and the church has agreed to pick up the tab. Not only that, but a dozen families in the church, on a regular stand-by basis, will serve Sunday dinner to any college student who wants a home-cooked meal.

Southern California

Growing churches like these are thrilling to see. It lifts Christian faith to recognize God's hand at work through His people in so many different places and in so many different ways. If you were to come to Southern California, you would want to attend the spectacular drive-in service at Garden Grove Community Church with its sliding glass wall and twelve decorative fountains.

And you could go to Melodyland Christian Center and feel the pulse of thousands of Spirit-filled Christians celebrating their faith.

You would love to see Calvary Chapel, which began its unusual growth as a center of the Jesus People movement in the 1960s.[1]

Next you will want to visit Grace Community Church in Panorama City where their new auditorium is already packed with over 2,500 persons who come out on Sunday morning, principally to hear the hour-long Bible exposition from Pastor John MacArthur.

Then attend a service at Bel Air Presbyterian Church, a spectacular piece of architecture—built on the edge of a cliff overlooking Los Angeles—where Pastor Donn Moomaw's flock is adding between 100 and 200 new members per year.

25

Some Grow and Some Do Not

I could go on and on citing other examples of growing churches. But these I have mentioned already are sufficient to indicate that some churches in the United States and Canada are indeed growing. Pastors and people in them are excited about being Christians and working for God. The Lord is adding daily such as should be saved—even as He did in the First Church of Jerusalem described in the book of Acts.

Just what is it that makes some churches grow?

And why are other churches dead on the vine? For it is a fact that many churches are dead. They haven't grown in years. For every new family that comes in, two or three go out. Attending church is a chore—something to get over with as soon as possible before settling down to a more enjoyable activity like watching the pro football game on television.

Statistics from a year ago show that some whole denominations are growing while others are declining. From one year to the next, for example, the Christian and Missionary Alliance, the Church of God (Cleveland), the Nazarenes, the Assemblies of God, the Baptist General Conference, the Southern Baptists and others all grew well, while during the same year the United Methodists, the Disciples of Christ, the Episcopalians, the United Presbyterians, the American Baptists and others declined.

But even that pattern is not uniform. Many Methodist, Presbyterian and American Baptist churches are growing, and many Alliance, Nazarene and Southern Baptist churches are losing membership.

Sometimes these churches are close to one another. In case after case struggling, discouraged churches find themselves within only two or three blocks of sister churches which are thriving. It is not uncommon in America for church members to drive past a half dozen other churches to get to the church of their choice. And that church doesn't differ one iota in doctrine from many of the other churches they pass, but their own church has something the others don't seem to have.

There are no particular regions of America that can be considered the promised land for growth. I used to think that California was the place where churches grew like dandelions on a golf course while New England was barren soil. I now realize it is much more complex than that. Southern Baptist churches, for example, are growing much more rapidly in New England than in California, although ten years ago it was the other way around. California may have more than its share of flamboyant, headline-grabbing churches, but when it comes to statistics, California has a higher percentage of unchurched people than New England!

Why? Why? Why?

Is there any sense to all this?

Why do some churches grow while others do not?

The answer to this question is so elusive that many churchmen even hesitate to raise it.

Back in the 1960s, as most of us remember all too well, many had even begun to question whether the church *should* grow. There was a doubt in some minds as to whether the church could ever be a benefit to society as a whole. For a while it became fashionable in certain circles to proclaim that we now live in a "post-Christian age."

Some overhang from the 1960s still persists like a pesky cough after a hard cold. But by and large, church growth has edged up toward the top of the agenda in churches across the board. The Baptist General Conference, for example, has just launched a growth program called "Double in a Decade." They have the faith to believe that their membership will move from 115,000 to 230,000 by 1985.

The Evangelical Covenant churches have recently rallied around a "Giving for Growing" project to the tune of contributing several million dollars over and above their regular church commitment. They definitely want Covenant churches to grow. Some Presbyterian and Episcopalian churches are requesting church growth seminars, dissatisfied with their present trends.

Yes, few people are making jokes about the Church these days. Most Christians are dead serious about their churches. Where they are growing, people are excited and anxious to do their part to keep things moving for the glory of God. Where they are declining, people want to know the reasons why and what they can do about it.

Finding the answers to the question of why churches are growing or not growing is what the Church Growth Movement is all about. No one has the final word, but good answers are surfacing with increasing frequency.

There are many different ways of approaching the task of discovering what God is doing in today's world. And one of them—as we are doing here—is to look around the country at the churches that seem to be doing something unusual and, consequently, are maintaining a steady pattern of growth. And while we look at them, we ask again our original question: *Just what is it that makes churches like these grow?*

Of course, it is, in the final analysis, God at work through His Holy Spirit. But if we study these churches and others like them more closely, we can learn more about God and the way He works.

You see, if I need to study harvesting procedures, I want to be where production is "thirty, sixty and one hundred fold," as the Bible says (see Matt. 13:8). By the same token, if I want to learn more about why churches grow, I can hardly do better than to study growing churches.

How They Do It

Others also believe we can learn from these churches. In fact, many of the pastors of growing churches have received so many calls for help that they have organized how-we-do-it seminars— held one to four times a year on their church campuses. Every March, for example, Pastor Jack Hyles of First Baptist, Hammond holds a Pastors' School. In 1974 the school drew 2,311 participants and in 1975 it drew 3,914.

Pastor Robert Schuller of Garden Grove Community Church limits enrollment in his Institute for Successful Church Leadership

28

to 220, but rarely is Wilbert Eichenberger, director of the Institute, able to hold to that number.

Undoubtedly the best training course in the country for techniques of personal evangelism is the Evangelism Explosion clinic at the Coral Ridge Presbyterian Church. Just recently, a year-long course of study has been inaugurated, and a new center for training is being developed in England.

Pastor Jerry Falwell of Thomas Road Baptist Church, Lynchburg, Virginia, holds an annual Pastors' School and Workers' Conference. In 1972 he drew more than 5,600.

In Fresno, California, G. L. Johnson, Pastor of People's Church, conducts a Fall seminar on Church Management and Christian Leadership.

W. A. Criswell, pastor of First Baptist, Dallas, Texas, covers every area of ministry in his annual School of the Prophets.

Ray Stedman teaches the body life principles of Peninsula Bible Church, Palo Alto, California, in a two-week internship program.

The tuition costs for these non-academic training opportunities run from $20 to $200. And though they will never substitute for a seminary education, they certainly could receive more of a place in ministerial training than they have up to the present time.

Church Growth Is Complex

Even when we put together all that is taught in these seminars, we recognize that we still have a great deal to learn about why some churches grow and some don't. Simply put, *church growth is complex*. There is no way it can be reduced to a simple formula or a canned program.

W. A. Criswell, for example, credits the growth of First Baptist, Dallas, largely to expository preaching of the Word. But Robert Schuller rarely preaches an expository message. His topical messages communicate "possibility thinking" to unbelievers who know nothing about the Bible and care little whether they do.

James Kennedy will single out house-to-house visitation as the most effective means for growth in Florida, but Stephen Olford tried it in New York City to no avail. He depends more on penetrating the high-rises through television.

Richard Halverson finds that developing small koinonia groups is his best approach in Washington D.C. Wendell Belew of the Southern Baptist Home Mission Board, however, once told me of two churches that "died of koinonia"!

Jack Hyles argues that building his Sunday School through busing helps his whole church grow, but Ray Ortlund's church sold its last Sunday School bus three years ago and has been growing faster ever since.

Qualities of Church Growth Leaders

While the patterns of church growth in America and elsewhere may be complex, they are not chaotic. A considerable degree of expertise is accumulating among those who have entered the field of church growth on a professional basis. And those who do so usually have combined a certain set of personal qualities which give a kind of identity to church growth leaders.

Here are five of them. In other words, if you meet a church growth leader, you can recognize him or her by:

1. *Single-minded obedience.* Church growth leaders take the Lordship of Jesus Christ very seriously. They have counted, as Dietrich Bonhoeffer would say, "the cost of discipleship." They are willing to pay the price for doing whatever is necessary to obey and fulfill God's Great Commission (Matt. 28:19-20). They are fully aware that a steward's faithfulness will ultimately be evaluated by the result of his efforts, and they have a deep desire to hear those coveted words on the last day: "Well done, thou good and faithful servant" (Matt. 25:21, *KJV*).

2. *Clearly defined objectives.* Church growth leaders are motivated by the assurance that they have understood the revealed will of God for world evangelization and that they are attuned to what God expects to accomplish through them. Thus, they are not reluctant to set measurable goals and to allow their success

30

or failure to be evaluated in the light of these goals, risky as this procedure might seem to some.

They have long since rejected counting "decisions" or those who "pray to receive Jesus" as criteria for evaluating evangelistic success. They are interested only in *disciples,* validated primarily through commitment to Jesus Christ as Lord and to responsible membership in a Christian church.

3. *Reliance on discerning research.* Church growth leaders are well aware of what must have been behind the words of Proverbs 18:13 (*TLB*): "What a shame—yes, how stupid!—to decide before knowing the facts." All too much Christian work is undertaken stupidly simply because the facts of the situation are not adequately known.

Present research methodology leaves much room for improvement; nevertheless, substantial advances have been made in the field. More and more is becoming known about how to plan intelligently for church growth, and research efforts are being accelerated.

4. *Ruthlessness in evaluating results.* Church growth leaders have often been criticized as being too pragmatic. They are pragmatic, but they would like to consider it as *consecrated* pragmatism.

If methods currently being used for some evangelistic effort, for example, are not accomplishing the stated goals, they must be revised or scrapped. A strategy must be substituted that will produce the results that God desires.

Church growth is an activist's philosophy. Little wonder that those who prefer to be passive and "leave the results to God" argue that shrinking churches are likely to be the most faithful churches and write books like Robert Hudnut's *Church Growth Is Not the Point.*[2] It goes without saying that such a thesis is unacceptable to church growth people.

5. *An attitude of optimism and faith.* Church growth leaders are not intimidated by the charge that they are "triumphalists." They are convinced that Christ is building His Church as He said He would (see Matt. 16:18), and they are confident that the gates of hell will not prevail against it. They are excited about

31

participating in the building of the Church worldwide and they rejoice when churches grow and multiply.

They pray for conversions in large numbers. They expect God to bring about people movements to Christ. Their New Testament pattern for evangelism is not the rich young ruler, but the day of Pentecost where 3,000 came to Christ and "continued steadfastly in the apostles' doctrine and fellowship, and in breaking of bread, and in prayers" (Acts 2:42, *KJV*). They believe that this is pleasing to God because it is a product of faith.

What Are the Vital Signs?

When the mentality generated by the kind of personal characteristics just described is put to use many interesting things happen. For one thing, sick churches become healthy churches. And healthy churches, like healthy people, exhibit certain vital signs. If the Church is the body of Christ, then there is some biblical justification in taking a rather clinical approach to analyzing the health of a church.

Human vital signs include pulse, respiration, blood pressure and temperature. If my temperature registers 98.6°, I know it is a sign of health. And I know this is so because medical researchers have taken the temperatures of enough healthy people to determine "normal temperature." Enough data has since been accumulated by medical science so that diagnosis of health or illness is, in many cases, rather routine.

But what then are the vital signs of a healthy church? Here are seven such indicators of ecclesiastical good health:

1. *The pastor.* What kind of a role must the pastor play if the church is to grow?

2. *The people of the church.* Is it possible for a church to grow if it has a perfect kind of pastor, but the wrong kind of people? How can the wrong kind of people become the right kind of people?

3. *Church size.* How big does a church need to be in order to be healthy and growing?

4. *Structure and functions.* How can a church be so structured

32

that all of its primary functions are operating at peak efficiency?

5. *Homogeneous unit.* Is it important that a church be composed of basically one kind of people, or should it be a mixture of races and classes?

6. *Methods.* What kinds of methods have proved to be effective instruments for evangelism in America today?

7. *Priorities.* How can the several good things that churches ought to do be arranged in priority order according to biblical principles and effectiveness for growth?

But before we zero in for a closer look at these vital signs we need first to ask one more question: Is the whole philosophy of church growth which causes us to ask all these questions pleasing to God?

Let's answer that last question first, shall we?

STUDY QUESTIONS

1. What did you learn from the examples of growing churches given in the text? Do you agree that there is no one method or one place where the Church can grow?

2. What do you think about the set of personal qualities that are outlined by the author concerning church growth leaders? Do you feel that your pastor has any of these qualities? If so, which ones are the most significant towards church growth?

3. What are the author's vital signs for church growth? Again, do you feel that your church has these? If so, which ones are functioning to the full benefit of the Church?

Footnotes

1. The story of Calvary Chapel is told in a book by Chuck Smith with Hugh Steven, *The Reproducers* (Glendale, California: G/L Publications, 1972).
2. Robert Hudnut, *Church Growth Is Not the Point* (New York: Harper and Row, 1975).

what is church growth all about?

At one time—before I met him—I thought Donald McGavran was an outright quack. What I had read in his *Church Growth Bulletin* was totally different from what I had learned previously. So I had a hard time understanding why my alma mater, Fuller Theological Seminary, invited *that* man to set up its School of World Mission.

Why? I had been turned off by McGavran's terminology!

Such terms as "scientific principles," "new philosophy," "theoreticians," "practitioners," and "professionals in the field" are uncommon vocabulary in most discussions of the Lord's work. And this unfamiliar language of the Church Growth Movement raises questions in the minds of many dedicated Christian people.

Is this church growth approach really spiritual or might it be carnal?

Is there anything in God's Word that tells us we need to be "scientific" in bringing people to Christ?

Is there not a danger that sociology and computers may subtly take the place of the Holy Spirit?

In a word, does all this please God?

I know these questions are real because I was asking them myself when I first came, during my second missionary furlough from Bolivia, to study at Fuller under McGavran. Frankly, I entered his program in 1967 as a skeptic. But I emerged an enlightened person.

I had sipped from the fountainhead of what was to become a major stream of influence on the mission fields of the world. And I now believe this same stream will flow with equal significance here in America.

If I were not convinced that the church growth approach is true to God's Word and pleasing to Him, I personally would have no part of it. But neither do I think less of those good people who have tried it and don't like it. Never for a moment would I say that, because they reject church growth thinking, they are thereby displeasing God.

I may—and do—use my powers of persuasion to "enlighten" them, but all along I realize deep down that God may be able to use them better outside of the framework of church growth philosophy than within. And blessings on them! I believe firmly in Christian liberty—maximum freedom for each Christian to find the leading of the Holy Spirit for his life and to minister accordingly.

But what of us who have chosen to embrace the church growth school of thought? Are we ourselves on firm biblical ground?

Biblical Roots of Church Growth

The overall purpose of God for the unsaved people of the world is basic to New Testament Christianity and also to church growth. "The Son of man is come to seek and to save that which was lost," says Jesus Himself (Luke 19:10, *KJV*). The Lord is longsuffering, Peter adds, "not willing that any should perish, but that all should come to repentance" (2 Pet. 3:9, *KJV*).

If these two verses were just isolated proof texts they might

35

not be sufficient to establish the premise for a major movement. But they are not. The God we see in the Bible is a seeking and a finding God.

Immediately after Adam and Eve ate the forbidden fruit and fell into sin, God called out to Adam in the garden, "Where art thou?" (Gen. 3:9, *KJV*). Ever since then, He has actively been seeking people separated from Him by sin. He was so serious about it that He finally sent "his only begotten Son, that whosoever believeth in him should not perish, but have everlasting life" (John 3:16, *KJV*).

The provision God has made for bringing lost people to Himself is the gospel. This is the good news that Jesus commanded to be preached to every creature (see Mark 16:15). It is the gospel that Paul preached in power to the Thessalonians (see 1 Thess. 1:5) and that turned them "to God from idols to serve the living and true God" (1 Thess. 1:9, *KJV*). The difference between those who perish and those who are saved is their response to the gospel. Thus, it is crucial that all lost people in the world hear the gospel and hear it in such a way that they will repent of their sins and place their trust and commitment in Christ as their Lord.

For reasons impossible to understand fully, God has not chosen to make the gospel known all by Himself. No question that He could do it if He wanted to, but instead He has chosen to use Christian people to do the job.

"Whosoever shall call upon the name of the Lord shall be saved," the Bible says. But then it goes on to add, "How then shall they call on him in whom they have not believed? and how shall they believe in him of whom they have not heard? and how shall they hear without a preacher?" (Rom. 10:13,14 *KJV*).

No way!

This implies that we human beings have a tremendously important responsibility in the execution of God's plan for the world. We may wish we didn't have to shoulder so much responsibility, but we cannot shirk it if we are serious about calling Jesus "Lord."

The New Testament frequently reminds us that we are "stewards

36

of God." In biblical times, the steward was the person placed in charge of the affairs of his master. If the steward goofed, the master lost out, but the steward also paid the price (see Matt. 25: 26-29).

The Bible clearly says that "it is required in stewards, that a man be found faithful" (1 Cor. 4:2, *KJV*). Faithful stewardship involves using all possible resources in accomplishing the will of the master. When this is done successfully, the steward is called "good and *faithful*" (Matt. 25:21, *KJV*).

Paul considered himself a "steward of the mysteries of God" (see 1 Cor. 4:1). He was entrusted with the *gospel*, even as we are. And Christians whose ministry is guided by a church growth philosophy take this stewardship very seriously.

The Master wants lost men and women found and saved. He expects His stewards to accomplish this objective and provides them with an all-important resource for doing it, namely the Holy Spirit. Jesus' disciples were told to tarry in Jerusalem "until ye be endued with power from on high" (Luke 24:49, *KJV*).

The disciples waited and prayed. But once they were endued, they didn't wait any more. They exploded into action on the day of Pentecost, and church growth began right there and then. It grew from 120 to 3,120 in one day, and every day after that it grew some more (see Acts 2:47).

The Spirit-filled steward is expected to use all his own resources to serve the Master: time, money and energy. And God wants it all used for His glory. Ironically, however, some conscientious Christians who are faithful stewards of their time and money are shy about using energy, particularly mental energy.

Without saying it in so many words, these Christians tend to think that the more a person is filled with the Holy Spirit the less he has to use his mind. So, for them, the converse is also true: the more a person uses his mind, the less spiritual he is. This kind of person usually has real problems in accepting the church growth point of view.

God delights to "guide us with his eye." We are not to be like "the horse or the mule which have no understanding" (see

Ps. 32:8,9). The difference between humans and animals is that God made humans in His own image with minds that are rational. That's why Jesus was able to tell His followers that they were to love the Lord with all their *minds* as well as with their other faculties (see Matt. 22:37).

Science in God's Service

Using the mind well to understand, plan and implement a specific task brings science into the picture. If the book of Acts tells us anything, it tells us that the task God has entrusted to His stewards—us!—is to share the good news of the gospel with every person who is not yet a Christian, introduce that person to Jesus Christ, and bring him or her into active fellowship with other Christians in the church.

God wants Christians to be multiplied and He wants churches to be multiplied. The task is tremendous, and at the same time it is more complex than some might think. Sometimes God's work is well done, but sometimes it is a disaster.

What is the difference?

I recently heard a veteran missionary discuss this problem. He pointed out that in the old days in China some missionaries were doing a great job of evangelizing and planting new churches across the hills and plains of China. But others tried and tried and didn't succeed. He said that to them the answer for failure was invariably the same: "Go to Keswick."

It was assumed that all problems were ultimately spiritual. If only a Christian worker could get close to the Lord, if he could deepen his prayer life, if he studied the Word harder, if he "let go and let God,"—well, then God would bless, and he would become a successful church planter.

The only thing wrong with this theory, the missionary went on, was that it rarely worked in practice. More often than not this approach compounded an already existing guilt complex and wrought disastrous results. It either heightened the sense of failure so that the worker returned home in discouragement or so hardened the conscience of the person that he no longer worried about whether he had any results or not.

Theological ways were even developed to explain failure away. "Leave the results to God" was the most frequently used phrase. With this slogan the worker could finish out a difficult and sacrificial missionary career with very little fruit and never be concerned at all about whether he might have been able to do a better job if he had only changed the way he went about it.

I am altogether in favor of the kind of spiritual growth that takes place at Keswick, or in any other situation where a person meets God in a special way. Meeting God on a regular basis is Priority One in the life of a successful Christian worker. But to imagine that harvesters going into the whitened fields and coming out with empty arms at the end of the day is most likely a "spiritual problem" is, in my opinion, a dangerously simplistic approach. It is like hoping against hope that an automobile will fly if you just polish it enough or put high enough octane gasoline into the tank. No, to make an automobile fly will require much more complex changes.

The scientific aspect of church growth is vitally interested in understanding and describing all the factors which enter into cases of failure and success in evangelistic efforts. One of the factors, of course, is spiritual, but there are many more which also require explanation.

What Is Science All About?

And when you think of it, explaining phenomena is what all science is about. It is merely that science attempts to use appropriate language in explaining certain phenomena. Natural science tries to explain, for example, the organic composition of fossils or how an egg and sperm produce a fetus or what causes an eclipse of the moon. Social science tries to explain such phenomena as why women in our culture marry men like their fathers, why some Africans intentionally scar their faces or why the suicide rate is high among some groups and lower among others.

Church growth science follows suit. It tries to explain why some churches grow and others decline, why some Christians are able to bring their friends to Christ and into church membership and others are not or what are the symptoms of a terminal illness in a church.

The best of scientists in any field readily admit that all scientific knowledge is tentative. No scientific theories are ever proven, they just gain credibility and usefulness to the degree they are not *falsified.*

Scientists are always looking for better ways to explain the phenomena they study. For hundreds of years, for example, Ptolemy's theory of the universe was the best available scientific explanation of why the sun rises in the morning and sets in the evening. Then Copernicus offered a better theory which falsified Ptolemy's theory and has been useful ever since.

The germ theory of disease is a very useful one, but few believe that it is a totally adequate explanation of why some people get sick and some stay healthy. Newton's theories still explain many physical phenomena, but when matter and energy are shown to be interchangeable, they are no longer adequate. The reason Einstein became so famous is that his theory of relativity is able to explain many phenomena that had baffled scientists for centuries.

One of the great values of scientific theories is that as well as explaining the past they are useful in explaining the future. They help us know when a hurricane is approaching, what will happen to certain crops if lime and superphosphate are added to the soil or whether a deep hole in a certain location is likely to strike oil.

In no case, however, does science explain all. The world is still waiting for more useful explanations for earthquakes, for the origin of cancer cells or for extrasensory perception.

Church Growth as a Science

All science ultimately has its origin in God. Scientific theories help us understand God's creation better. Yet for some reason or other, a scientific approach has not been used widely among

Christians for understanding God's work in the world with more precision. But church growth intends to do just that.

As a matter of curiosity, none of the members of the faculty of the Fuller School of World Mission—where church growth theory has been generated to date—has his doctorate in theology or philosophy as such. Rather, faculty members combine such academic fields as civil engineering, education, social ethics, linguistics, agriculture and anthropology where scientific methodology is a prominent part of the training. Of course, each one has done his basic graduate work in theology—B.D., MDiv., ThM., but this is combined with a scientific approach not usually stressed in either theological seminary or liberal arts college. The result is a new, and presumably useful, way of looking at what God is doing in the world.

Church growth science provides a new frame of reference from which to interpret old phenomena. Even though it claims no absolute "laws," it is valuable in that the theories that emerge sensitize us to see things that we never would have seen otherwise. It provides a new language, new labels and new models for increasing our effectiveness as God's stewards.

Church growth as a science helps us maximize the use of energy and other resources for God's greater glory. It enables us to detect errors and correct them before they do too much damage. It would be a mistake to claim too much, but some enthusiasts feel that with church growth insights we may even step as far ahead in God's task of world evangelization as medicine did when aseptic surgery was introduced.

Lack of church growth is a serious disease, but in most cases it is a curable one. The cure, however, is usually not simple. More often it requires as careful a diagnosis and therapy as a tumor on the ovary or a coronary thrombosis. One of the central tasks of the church growth school is (1) to develop scientific techniques of diagnostic research for ailing churches and (2) to design instruments to be used in the kind of therapy which will restore normal church health.

Just as in medicine, it will take specialized and professional training to use these new tools well. Sometimes a stomach ache can be cured at home. But when Pepto-Bismol and Alka-2 fail, most people decide to seek the advice of a professional. This has not been true in our churches to any great extent, because few such professionals were available. But specialists are now being trained and equipped to give much more than superficial answers to the question, "Why isn't my church growing?"

How Can a Church Grow?

How to correct stagnation and decline in the church has become a high priority concern across the board in the America of the 1970s. More and more, as I travel across the country, I hear concerned laymen, pastors and denominational executives asking the same question: "What can we do to make our church grow?"

In the process of searching for answers to that question, I will be the first to admit that I am not nor have I ever been the pastor of a healthy, growing church. My self-identity is more that of an objective, scientific researcher. As such I have some disadvantages, but also some advantages.

It may not be obvious at first, but it is a fact that many pastors of growing churches have only slim insight into the reasons why their churches are growing. They have difficulty in seeing the forest for the trees. For example, I always include on my students' reading lists a particular book describing the growth of one very large and very prominent church in America. In it the pastor of that church writes ten chapters, each one describing what he perceives to be one of the major reasons why his church is growing. But when my students—who are themselves pastors—write reviews of the book, very frequently they comment that they still don't know why this church grows. Most of the ten reasons, they say, could be used to describe many shrinking churches they know of.

McGavran, for example, tells of interviewing one pastor of a growing church who gave as the principal reason for its growth: "We preach the Bible as the Word of God and are faithful to it." Then McGavran later asked another pastor why he thought his church had *not* grown for the last ten years. The answer: "We preach the Bible as the Word of God and are faithful to it."

The application is obvious.

Sometimes talking to pastors of growing churches reminds me of reading the stories of people who live to be 100. Particularly in a small town, the town newspaper will interview any of the citizens who celebrates his or her 100th birthday. Invariably one of the questions is, "What did you do to live so long?"

One person will say, "I lived a clean life, never drank and never smoked." But in the next town the centenarian will say, "The only thing that has kept me going this long has been a pint of whiskey a day and a box of cigars a week!"

Neither of them knew with any kind of accuracy why he had lived that long because neither had been trained to think scientifically about his life span. And most pastors have not been trained to think scientifically. Some pastors do have an excellent grasp on the growth dynamics of their church and are able to communicate them to others. But not too many.

Yet the vital signs of healthy churches are there, and somehow they need to be described in ways that are both intrinsically accurate and helpful to others. The person who does this must study a number of churches across the board, not just the one he is directly involved in. In order to do this best, the researcher must be relatively free on Sundays—the day churches do their most serious business. Most pastors are limited in the number of Sundays they get to spend in other churches during a typical year.

I am free on Sundays in a sense that most pastors are not. So I have visited dozens of churches and interviewed scores of pastors in the conduct of my research. I have also read countless articles and books and graded hundreds of term papers analyzing the growth of American and Canadian churches.

In describing the seven vital signs of healthy churches as I have perceived them, I do not claim finality in my conclusions. Church growth is still a young science, and new developments

43

are breaking all the time. Yet it should be said here that there is no simple formula for producing instant church growth.

If your church is not growing and you would like it to grow, it will require prayer, study, hard work and—above all—faith.

So let's begin at the beginning—with faith!

STUDY QUESTIONS

1. What do you think about the author's biblical stand concerning church growth? Do you believe that it is profitable for scientists to work with church growth? Do you believe that the Bible teaches the practicality of using our minds and measuring what God is doing in the world?

2. Do you agree that a pastor could have a growing church and still not be able to explain why the church grows without some sort of scientific measurement?

is your faith big enough?

An essential ingredient in all Christian work is faith. The Bible tells us point-blank that "without faith it is impossible to please God" (see Heb. 11:6).

Faith on Display

In a recent church bulletin, Pastor Raymond Ortlund of Lake Avenue Congregational Church, Pasadena, California said to his congregation:

"There are over one million people living within 20 minutes' drive of Lake Avenue Church. When the freeway is completed the number will double. Most of these do not know Christ. We must share some of the responsibility to reach them for Christ. Some of them would not be open to us at all. But I estimate there are 50,000 who would respond to us and our style of ministry.

"One of my dreams is that by 1990 (15 years from now) at least 5,000 would be worshiping God here every Sunday morning. That means we must prayerfully prepare ourselves, our ministry, our facilities for these precious people.

"I also pray that we will begin several new congregations. I pray that we can minister to other churches and missions what God has taught us.

"What a tragedy if we let money or glass, steel and mortar

hinder our winning these lost to Christ and having a broad ministry for Him together.

"I am asking that you think about this. Commit yourself to Christ and to one another for this glorious mission. Nice, decent people will never make it. Only those who are totally given to Christ and to His Body of believers will do this kind of front-line work.

"Fresh commitment to Christ is first, but after that we love and sharpen each other for growth together. Then God, who calls the signals, will tell us 'when' for each step ahead.

"God bless you. Let's go for God!"

Ortlund's statement is tremendously significant in that as he looks 15 years ahead to 1990 he sees his own church attendance at 5,000—more than double current attendance, he sees several new churches like his in the area and he sees other churches which are not growing now coming to life and beginning to grow as a result of his ministry.

All this is a formidable public display of *faith*. According to Hebrews 11:1 (*KJV*), "Faith is the substance of things hoped for, the evidence of things not seen." Because Pastor Ortlund, through the eyes of faith, can see 5,000 people praising God on the Lake Avenue Church campus, he can realistically face such things as how much money, glass, steel and mortar it will take. This is the kind of attitude that pleases our Lord.

Jesus and Faith

Jesus, time after time, taught His disciples the necessity of exercising faith. Matthew tells the story of a man who had a son with epilepsy. Jesus' disciples tried to cure him, but they failed. Then Jesus cast the demon out and the child was cured instantly.

Afterward, the disciples asked why He could do it, while they couldn't. "Because of your unbelief," Jesus said. "If ye have faith as a grain of mustard seed, . . . nothing shall be impossible unto you" (Matt. 17:20, *KJV*).

On another occasion Peter decided that if Jesus could walk on water, so could he. He started out to do it and it worked!

46

But soon he lost his nerve and started to sink. What were Jesus' words of rebuke? "O thou of little faith" (Matt. 14:31, *KJV*).

As Jesus looks over His present-day disciples, particularly those whom He is holding responsible as stewards of the resources that should be used for church growth, He must frequently say, "O ye of little faith."

The Indispensable Condition

Without faith it is impossible to please God. Likewise without faith it is impossible for churches to grow. If Christian people do not look ahead in faith and see their church growing, it will not grow.

Faith involves setting goals in terms of things hoped for and things unseen. Or, as Edward Dayton says, "Every goal is a statement of faith." So a goal of 5,000 by 1990 is a direct and intentional exercise of faith.

Remember, *the indispensable condition for a growing church is that it wants to grow.* This does not mean, of course, that a church will grow by just wanting to. But if it doesn't want to grow, it will not grow. And if it is a growing church, it wants to grow. Wanting to grow and planning for growth is another way of applying biblical faith.

Remnant Theology

It is a fact that some Christians do not want their church to grow. They are unimpressed by biblical and theological arguments for church growth. Somehow they have learned to rationalize their lethargy toward winning the lost to Christ, although with their lips they would deny that they are lethargic.

These believers have designed what McGavran calls a "remnant theology," and they take a certain satisfaction in being a minority despised by unbelievers. They consider their unattractiveness a virtue and enjoy being described as "separate from the world."

Two Levels of Faith: The Pastor

The exercise of faith for church growth must come on two

47

levels. First, the pastor must want his church to grow. The most formidable obstacle to growth that I know of is a pastor who thinks negatively and who is pessimistic about growth opportunities in his community. Such a pastor teaches that the basic task of the church is to care for those sheep already in the fold rather than to concentrate on winning lost sheep and constantly incorporating new ones into the flock.

It is true that some ministers simply are not equipped psychologically to handle a church larger than a one-person operation. One minister is usually adequate for a church of one or two hundred members. When the church is below that level, that kind of a pastor may work hard for growth and perhaps attain it.

When the church reaches a certain point, however, and when some begin suggesting that the staff might need to be increased, a threat arises and the pastor may begin—without publishing it in the bulletin!—to plan for zero growth. And it is altogether possible that this may be done unconsciously without either the pastor or the lay leaders really understanding what is taking place in their church.

This kind of unexpansive personality has a place in church growth. What he can do, he probably can do well. He is a servant of God. But he needs a structure where he can pastor a congregation—not necessarily a church—without feeling the threat of being overtaken by something he is incompetent to handle or without feeling guilty because he is so threatened.

If placed in the proper structure, he can become an asset rather than a liability to church growth. One of the immediate challenges to church growth specialists is to identify and describe just such a structure and to work out procedures whereby pastors of this type can be painlessly shifted into more productive positions. Intuitively I know that such a structure exists.

Two Levels of Faith: The Laity

The second level on which faith must be exercised for church growth is with the people of the church. The lay leaders in particular must want their church to grow. If they do not, they can effectively and almost effortlessly prevent it.

Christian Closed Shops

One of the chief causes for a negative attitude on the part of laymen is that the congregation has become almost like an extended family. They have grown to know and love each other so much that they would feel extremely uncomfortable if an outsider were to penetrate the inner circle. Again this is often unconscious, but an outsider soon gets the message that he is not fully welcome and will not stay around the church very long under those conditions.

There are other causes as well. An undue stress on Christian perfection can turn a congregation into spiritual navel-gazers who are so pleased with their own heroic attainments that they have little tolerance for newer Christians who are not as polished. They are somewhat like middle-aged couples who detest the thought of changing diapers and all that goes with it, and who carefully practice birth control to avoid that possibility.

Again, a congregation full of bickering and backbiting also becomes very self-centered. So much energy is spent on trying to hold the internal pieces together and to survive that little attention is given to winning the lost. Even if some were won, they would not find there the atmosphere for healthy Christian growth and would likely shop around for a more satisfying church home. Worse yet, they might end up "spiritual orphans."

Faith Plus Works

But suppose that the pastor and the laymen all do want the church to grow. It has already been mentioned that this in itself is not enough to assure growth. The faith might be there, but as the Epistle of James asserts, "faith without works is dead" (James 2:20, *KJV*). In that light then, I expand my former statement to say that the *indispensable condition for a growing church is that it wants to grow and is willing to pay the price for growth.*

Robert Schuller warns that "if you fail to plan you plan to

fail." Growth happens only in churches that plan for growth. And an essential part of planning includes anticipating the cost.

Church growth costs time. A church of 2,000 is ever so much more demanding than a church of 200. It costs energy. It might mean two or three sermons on a Sunday morning rather than one. It means more and longer board meetings. It means planning sessions and long-range task forces.

And it costs money. True, the new members will help pay the bills, but the key decisions for growth must be taken even before new people come into the picture, and thus they require a considerable measure of faith.

This very practical corollary of faith must not be slighted or overlooked. It is easy to do. It is easy to assume that if through the teaching of the Word the congregation develops high enough levels of faith, love, hope, prayer and worship, then growth will come spontaneously.

Spontaneous growth is a pleasant dream, but not much more. Planning for growth and agreeing to pay the price for growth is much more realistic. Even growing churches which claim spontaneous growth, upon analysis, will usually reveal a significant degree of planning below the surface.

The "Church on the Grow"

Pastor Donald Hamman of the Medinah (Illinois) Baptist Church is well aware of growth dynamics. He and his people want to grow so much that they describe their church as the "church on the grow."

In a dramatic challenge for growth to his church in 1970, Hamman—sounding very much like Hebrews 11:1—reminded his people that moving forward would be a "venture into the unknown." He realistically predicted many "stumbles and mistakes" as they moved ahead together, but he was not afraid of risk. He had faith in God's power to carry them.

"But such progress does not come by chance," Hamman said. "It comes by setting primary goals and then by planning and programming to meet those goals."

50

Planned growth has paid top dividends in the Medinah Baptist Church. In ten years from the early 1960s to the early 1970s, when many churches in America were on the decline, the church grew from 85 to 300 members with a Sunday morning attendance of over 1,000.

A decadal growth rate of upwards of 250% is excellent for any church in any decade. Many churches would feel encouraged if they were growing at half or even one-quarter that rate.

Goals for Growth

Hamman would agree with Edward Dayton that "every goal is a statement of faith." Churches that really want to grow will set bold goals for growth.

The fact that relatively few churches do set goals is a sign that they are not as serious about wanting to grow as they say they are. They remind me of some of my overweight friends who feel very self-conscious about their size. These people are always talking about getting more exercise and going on a diet, but year after year they stay about the same. In my understanding, their actions prove they don't really *want* to lose weight, regardless of what they say.

Likewise, many evangelical churches tell everyone they want to grow, but they stay about the same year after year. Why? They fail to set bold goals and then do whatever is necessary to attain them.

Timidity Causes Failure

The chief deterrent to creative and courageous goal setting on the part of church leadership is timidity. Not to have goals, of course, is an extremely comfortable situation since with no goals it is impossible to fail.

No one wants to fail, and many have convinced themselves that failure can be avoided by aiming at nothing. It has rarely occurred to these timid souls that while their system disallows failure, it also disallows success.

So some who want to report success, but who fear risk, have

developed a very useful alternative technique of *talking* about goals. Their goals are whatever they happen to be doing at the time.

This method is fail-safe. It is like the marksman who shoots a bullet into the wall, then draws the target around the bullet hole.

Although this method of goal-setting can and does fool some people, it does not fool the Lord for one moment. He sees such people as adding to the already swollen number of "ye of little faith."

High Risks, High Returns

Taking a risk is part and parcel of exercising faith. This is clear in the parable of the talents, or thousands of dollars as *The Living Bible* has it. Notice that the businessman in the parable who gave his employees $5,000, $2,000 and $1,000 to invest respectively expected a high return on his investment.

The two "good and faithful servants" made a 100% return on the investment. Evidently this return was considerably above what the current rate of bank interest was, since the businessman told the "wicked and slothful servant" that the least he could have done with his money was put it in the bank (Matt. 25:27, *TLB*). But, as every businessman knows, a high return invariably involves a high risk.

God wants us to be bold. He wants us to take risks for Him. He expects a high return from His stewards.

The steward who buried his money had no goal except to avoid failure. He admitted, "I was afraid" (Matt. 25:25, *TLB*). And what did his timidity gain him?

Failure!

Lack of faith is always and inexorably self-defeating.

Possibility Thinking

No one that I know is more eloquent in deriding lack of faith on the part of church leaders than Pastor Robert Schuller. Faith is not just theory to him. He has built it into his very lifestyle.

In my judgment a staunch attitude of faith is the basic catalyst for the growth rate of over 500% per decade that the Garden Grove Community Church has maintained since it was first planted in 1955. Its membership of over 7,000 is ample evidence that hard at work there are some "good and faithful servants."

The point I want to make is that Pastor Schuller himself had to overcome a deep fear of failure in order to begin setting growth-stimulating goals. It happened when he fixed his attention on a slogan written across the top of a wall calendar: "I'd rather attempt to do something great and fail than attempt to do nothing and succeed." He allowed God to burn this concept into his soul, and it became one of the generating forces that produced his well-known philosophy of "possibility thinking."[1]

Possibility thinking boils down basically to a synonym of what the Bible calls "faith." Schuller's definition of possibility thinking is "the maximum utilization of the God-given powers of imagination exercised in dreaming up possible ways by which a desired objective can be attained." He is convinced that "the greatest power in the world is the power of possibility thinking."

"If your dream is from God," he adds, "then you need only to exercise this miracle-working power, and you can reach the seemingly unattainable goal!" Jesus continually tried to get this idea over to His disciples when He said, "If you have faith as a grain of mustard seed . . ." (Matt. 17:20, *KJV*).

Pastor Thomas Ray of Central Baptist Temple, Huntington Beach, California, is a possibility thinker. And his church is an example of outstanding growth. A former car salesman, Ray may well have learned the principles of goal-setting in the secular world.

God has consistently directed Ray into small, static churches where an infusion of possibility thinking is much needed. He first went into the Crestview Baptist Church in Irving, Texas where 25 people were still meeting in a home. Within five years Sunday School attendance had topped 600.

Then, six years ago, he was called to Central Baptist Temple. It was a struggling church of 50 people and deep in debt. Today the average attendance on Sunday is over 1,400.

How did it happen? It is a long story, but the climate was set in Pastor Ray's very first sermon of his ministry in Huntington Beach. He gathered his 50 members together and told them, "Nothing can keep us from growing, nothing!"

This was possibility thinking in action. But it has not ceased. Even though he now speaks to standing-room-only crowds, Pastor Ray still boldly proclaims, "We've got to double our attendance, double our buses, double our facilities, double our staff; but it will cost money—we've all got to double our giving!"[2]

Because it is so biblical, I remain convinced that without faith, it is impossible for churches to grow. Empirical evidence also validates the absolute necessity of faith or whatever else you want to call it—possibility thinking or goal-setting—as a prerequisite for church growth.

In other words, *the indispensable condition for a growing church is that it wants to grow and is willing to pay the price for growth.*

STUDY QUESTIONS

1. After reading this chapter, do you have a new perspective of faith as it relates to church growth? What are the two levels of faith discussed by the author? How could this relate to your responsibilities in your own church?

2. Is your church willing to grow and pay the price? If so, how could you measure your church's willingness? Illustrate.

3. The author is convinced that faith is an absolute necessity for church growth. Do you agree? Discuss this as a group.

Footnotes

1. How possibility thinking is directly related to church growth is described in fascinating detail in Robert Schuller's *Your Church Has Real Possibilities* (Glendale, California: G/L Publications, 1974).

2. Henry Lord, *Seven Successful Churches in Southern California,* unpublished dissertation, California Graduate School of Theology, 1975, p. 108.

pastor, don't be afraid of power!

In America, the primary catalytic factor for growth in a local church is the pastor. This may not be equally true in some other countries, especially where churches are multiplying much more rapidly than professional pastors can be trained and ordained. But here in America, there is in every growing, dynamic church a key person whom God is using to make it happen.

You can check this out for yourself. Just take a book like *Great Churches of Today*[1] or Elmer Towns' *America's Fastest Growing Churches*[2] and note the examples given of growing churches in the U.S. today. Almost without exception, these churches cited in these books have grown under the leadership of one person in particular to whom God has given special gifts and who is using these gifts to lead the church into growth.

Humility Says No

It is normal for the pastor of a growing church to deny that he is a primary key to growth. For one thing, this is due to sincere Christian humility. These pastors are men of God. They are acutely aware of the dangers of pride and haughtiness. They have preached to their congregations that "pride cometh before a fall" and they do not want to fall. They want God to have the glory and Jesus to be exalted. They are willing to decrease if Jesus can increase.

They also have profound respect for fellow ministers, many of whom are not experiencing growth at all in their churches. It is contrary to their sense of Christian graciousness to allow themselves to be placed in a position that might give the impression that they think themselves superior to other ministers and thus become alienated from them.

Furthermore, pastors of growing churches know they are not doing it alone, and they want to be the first to make this plain. Many of them work with a loyal and competent staff, and everybody is aware of the essential contribution that each staff member is making toward the growth of the church. No pastor desires to take credit for what a staff colleague is doing. So the pastor will frequently say, "Don't think I am responsible for this; I am just one member of a fantastic team."

And again, a good pastor will want to give due credit to his people. Where the pastor is the only staff member in smaller churches, if the small church is a growing church, the people in the congregation are pulling their weight. And no church, large or small, can grow well unless this happens.

The typical pastor, then, will be careful to make sure that the people of the congregation are well aware of his dependence on them, and he will remind them of it as often as possible. So as not to jeopardize the spiritual dynamic already at work among the people he will be very hesitant to accept public credit for the growth of the church.

It is true, then, that no pastor, regardless of how gifted he is, can make a church grow alone. The body of Christ was not

56

designed to function that way. From just the practical point of view, anyone could soon deduce that the only pastor who could possibly do all the work would be the pastor of a small church, but if that small church is *growing* it soon will be a church too big for any one person to do all the work involved. The larger a church grows, the less a share of the total work load the pastor himself can assume.

The People Love the Pastor

Vital Sign Number One of a healthy, growing church is a pastor who is a possibility thinker and whose dynamic leadership has been used to catalyze the entire church into action for growth. Interestingly enough, the first ones to recognize this are usually the members of the congregation themselves.

As I visit growing church after growing church I try to get the pulse of the average person in the pew as far as his or her attitude toward the pastor is concerned. Invariably I find a high degree of love and esteem for him. As a matter of fact, this is often exaggerated to the extent that many members of a growing church will claim—and sincerely so—that their pastor is the best pastor in the whole world.

How I love to hear that! Sometimes just to test it, I hint at a mild criticism of the pastor and watch the church member rise to his defense. When this happens, I know by that attitude alone that I am in a healthy church.

I compare such feelings to those in a happy family where the husband thinks his wife is the world's greatest and where the kids think there is no one like their dad. We smile when we hear a young child challenge a friend by saying, "My dad can lick your dad!" I also smile when I hear an adult Christian say—in effect, "My pastor can lick your pastor!"

Any outside observer knows that such statements are not based on objective facts. But this is unimportant. The important thing in this case is the *feeling* of the person who is involved in the church as an insider. Strong pastors of strong churches have earned

57

the fierce loyalty of their parishioners. The sheep love their shepherd.

A personal story here concerning my wife, Doris, and me will illustrate the point I am making about parishioner loyalty. One day, after I had received a very attractive offer for a position in a midwestern city, we played a game. By this time, of course, we had prayed about it and knew that God wanted us to stay in Pasadena, so the discussion took on a light tone.

We discussed the kids' schooling and how disruptive a move would be for them, but decided that they had moved many times before and could probably do it again. We thought of the cold winters and hot summers and the need for woolen clothing, fuel oil and anti-freeze, but thought if we had adapted to the jungles and mountains of Bolivia we could adapt again. We love our Spanish colonial house, but realized deep down that it was just another material possession that could never stand in the way of doing the will of God. We are stimulated by the ethnic diversity in our integrated community and did not relish moving into a blah, WASP small town, but if worse came to worse, we could make the adjustment.

To this point we were having fun. Then all of a sudden Doris' expression became serious and her eyes misted. I knew instantly the game was over.

"There's one thing we wouldn't have if we moved there," she said in a somber tone of voice. "Our pastor wouldn't be there, and he is something I for one am not at all prepared to consider giving up! No church in that other town could compare to ours."

I have thought about that incident many times because it pointed up—in a way very close to home for me—one of the dynamics of a growing church. Lake Avenue Congregational Church is the eighth church we have joined since we were converted twenty-five years ago. Of the eight, it is the first *growing* church we have been associated with.

We did not decide to join the church three years ago because of the pastor, although we were acquainted with him casually and had a good opinion of his ministry. We joined primarily because we thought our children would benefit from the youth program. What happened to us after we joined should happen to every Christian.

We felt welcome in the church, we felt enveloped with a genuine spirit of love and concern, we caught some of the excitement of growth and vitality, and in the midst of it all it gradually became evident to us that God was using one person above all others to make it happen—the pastor. Until Doris and I played our game, however, I had not realized how deep the feeling had become.

Authority Earned by Love

The kind of love that people in growing churches have for their pastor carries with it some implications that are not always recognized at first. One of these is that the pastor ends up with a great deal of authority. This is not some authority he has because of his ordination or erudition or job description. This is an authority that he has earned through relationships.

I have observed this fact of church life in Baptist and Nazarene and Presbyterian and Pentecostal churches. I have seen it in large churches and small churches, black churches and white churches. The pattern follows in Florida, New England, Texas and Indiana. The pastor of a growing church is typically a strong authority figure and that authority has been earned through living relationships with the people.

This is very similar to what often happens in a family situation. A father who loves his wife as Christ loved the church (Eph. 5:25) and who brings up his children in the nurture and admonition of the Lord (Eph. 6:4) often finds himself with a great deal of authority. His wife is willing to obey and fulfill his every wish and his children honor him and are in subjection.

Biblically, this is what a family ought to be like, and it is no mere coincidence that having proved that he can develop such a family situation is a prerequisite for church leadership in the Pastoral Epistles. A bishop, according to the apostle Paul, must rule his own house well and have his children in subjection, "For if a man know not how to rule his own house, how shall he take care of the church of God?" (1 Tim. 3:5, *KJV*).

When the head of a family has earned such authority, it often amazes outsiders. "I don't see how he gets away with what he does," some will comment. Others may say, "That woman is nothing but a slave!" Or even stronger, "He's a tyrant!" Those who have not lived it have a hard time understanding it.

A parallel situation exists in churches with pastors who have earned strong authority in the church. The church is—or *should* be—like a family. Frequently I have heard outsiders, particularly from non-growing churches, criticize the larger churches by saying something like: "They wouldn't be anywhere if it weren't for that one man."

"What will they do when they don't have Jack Hyles any more?"

"What will happen to the church when Schuller is gone?"

"If Jim Kennedy were to leave, the church would collapse!"

Because they are repeated so frequently, such statements must have some significance for those who use them. Yet members of these growing churches with wonderful pastors do not think this way themselves any more than most women who have wonderful husbands think they are bad off now because when their husbands die life will not be the same for them again. It is all too true, but it is not very important. The fact of the matter is that Hammond First Baptist *does* have Jack Hyles, Garden Grove Community *does* have Robert Schuller, Coral Ridge Presbyterian *does* have James Kennedy, and in these and numerous other churches like them unsaved people are being brought to Christ and into an exciting family of God!

Of course, the next generation will have to be saved, too, but it is not healthy for a church to spend too much time worrying about the next generation any more than it is healthy for a woman to spend too much time thinking about whom she will marry if her husband dies and leaves her a widow. The only generation any church is responsible for winning is this generation. The ripened harvest is ripe today, and the most important thing a church can do is what it is doing *now*.

Pastoral Longevity

One of the reasons why growing churches do not have to spend much time worrying about what will happen when their pastor goes is that a substantial number of pastors of growing churches have considered their particular parish to be a lifetime calling. They are not looking around for greener pastures.

Such pastors are excited about what they are doing, and they are fulfilled in their ministry. They love the people as much as the people love them. They do not regularly ask themselves, "Could it be that my ministry here is ending?" Pastors of growing churches are generally characterized by longevity in the ministry.

This principle of longevity does not apply only to the senior minister in a multiple staff church. In the healthiest situation it applies to everyone on the staff. Not all pastors have the gifts necessary to lead a church into prolonged growth. Many by nature are suited better for a subordinate role, and they are happy to work under a compatible senior minister for their whole lives. Strong staffs are built on this kind of person.

Beware of the person who accepts a staff position only as a stepping stone to a higher status or a larger church. Look for a minister of Christian education for whom Christian education is a lifetime area of specialization. Look for a youth minister who will be as capable of working with youth when he is 45 as when he was 25. Find a minister of visitation who will not get restless if he is not invited to take the pulpit frequently.

If a staff is built on the basis of spiritual gifts and calling to each particular position, it will be a strong one. Staff members under those circumstances will not tend to be jealous of or resent the authority of the senior pastor. In many social situations, including churches, there is usually room for only one person at the top. If all who are involved respect this truth and are content with their present situation, maximum progress can be made.

Pastoral Authority

Pastoral authority, earned through a loving relationship with the family of God, is thus an important ingredient for growth. To some it might appear as dictatorship or totalitarianism, but it is not. It is the recognition and exercise of God-given spiritual gifts in the body of Christ.

Some congregational-type churches oppose strong pastoral leadership on principle. Congregationalism was developed along with American democracy, and strong pastoral authority seems undemocratic to some Christians. Where this feeling persists, it will be overcome if the church wants to move into a pattern of growth.

Medinah Baptist Church

Pastor Donald Hamman of Medinah Baptist Church became strongly aware of this problem in a congregational-type church. Medinah Baptist—the "church on the grow"—with a current membership of around 300, is a church relatively easy to identify with in comparison with Schuller's 7,000, Hyles' 32,000 or Kennedy's 3,000.

Composite Membership

Before describing Pastor Hamman's leadership style, it would be well to know more about the church. Ten years ago in 1964, the church had 85 members. At the end of 1974, it had 300. But in this case, the communicant membership does not tell the whole story. It is much more useful in the case of Medinah Baptist—and elsewhere in America, across the board—to use the relatively new category of "composite membership" as the data base for analyzing church growth.

The composite membership factor was first introduced by Charles Mylander in 1975.[3] Mylander found that membership statistics alone were not very useful in comparing the growth of four Friends churches in Orange County, California. So he experimented with several formulas and finally concluded that a combination of membership, worship attendance and Sunday School attendance gave a much more accurate picture.

Composite membership is calculated by adding (1) the membership at the end of the year—however the particular church chooses to define membership; (2) the average worship attendance for the year—leave Christmas and Easter in, for they will usually be counterbalanced by the "summer slump"; and (3) the average Sunday School attendance—Sunday School enrollment is probably less realistic than attendance. Then divide the total by three to get the composite membership figure.

At the end of 1974 the membership of Medinah Baptist was 300, the worship service averaged slightly over 1000 and the Sunday School also was slightly over 1000. This gives a composite membership of 767. In 1964 the composite membership was 198. Over that decade, then, the composite growth rate of the church was 287%.

How Fast Is Fast Growth?

Now, without a point of comparison, such a figure is meaningless. Is a 287% decadal growth rate good, bad or indifferent? In other words, *how fast is fast growth?*

Biological Growth

A rule of thumb established years ago by Donald McGavran states that *biological growth* should be calculated on the basis of 25% per decade. *Biological growth occurs when the children of believers are raised in a Christian way, taught about Jesus, converted and incorporated into church membership.*

It is obvious that the 25% figure would vary according to the population growth of the particular region in which the church is located, but much experimentation has shown that more precise calculations do not ultimately help the analysis. Use the 25% per decade as a starting point for thinking of church growth. In other words, if a church is growing at only 25% per decade, it is barely growing at all.

In the U.S.A. (other countries might differ), a decadal growth rate of 50% is not too bad. Not really healthy perhaps, but not unhealthy either. A church growing at 100% per decade is in pretty good shape. If it shows 200%, the church is newsworthy, and when the figure gets up around 300% the pastor better prepare to hold seminars to share his methods with others. For sure, he is doing something very significant.

So this gives us a handle to understand that the growth rate of 287% per decade in the Medinah Baptist Church is excellent. Before going on, however, notice that when analyzing the growth of a church, the bottom line should be expressed in *rates* of growth, not in absolute numbers. This method will soon deflate inflated membership statistics and keep everybody involved honest and out of the "numbers game." It also provides a uniform way of comparing otherwise differing churches across the board.

Medinah Baptist is growing extremely well. It has many things going for it. It has a good location in a Chicago suburb, the population is growing, the congregation is devoted and hard working. However, the leadership of Donald Hamman has been decisive. One observer describes him as "a capable, spiritual, intelligent, analytical, industrious, loving leader with gifts of evangelist, pastor and teacher."[4]

Are Committees Clumsy?

On February 8, 1970, Hamman exercised his constitutional privilege of calling a special church business meeting. He knew intuitively that the church had reached a crucial point for its growth, so he prepared what he called a "Crossroads Message" for his people. In it, he laid his own future as pastor of the church on the line.

With a Sunday morning attendance of 450, he felt that the church had begun to feel self-satisfied and was ready to settle with the status quo. Hamman's godly restlessness would not tolerate such an attitude. In his message he demanded that the church push forward to new growth with the objective of "becoming the unquestioned Gospel-preaching evangelistic center in the entire metropolitan Chicago area."

Combined with this God-sized dream was an enviable touch of realism. Hamman felt that, like most churches he knew, Medinah Baptist was programmed and structured for mediocrity.

"Our bulky bureaucracy of committees is a hindrance to action," he declared. He felt that committees were too often an excuse for busyness rather than vehicles for decisive planning. He described committee work as "much deliberation, considerable aggravation, unnecessary tensions and very little action!"

So he went on to reason with the congregation about his role as a leader. First he asked them if they really trusted him. Did they trust his doctrinal purity, his financial integrity, his moral uprightness, his unfeigned love of the brethren and his dedication to the work?

The congregation knew him well, and their answers to all the questions were positive. He had *earned* their love and respect.

Having established this, he then asked for a fresh mandate as their leader. "If you believe God has called me to pastor this church," he asked, "then will you follow me?"

He likened the total church to an army. This army has only one Commander-in-Chief, Jesus Christ. The local church is like a company with one company commander, the pastor, who gets his orders from the Commander-in-Chief. The company commander has lieutenants and sergeants under him for consultation and implementation, but the final responsibility for decisions is that of the company commander, and he must answer to the Commander-in-Chief.

In effect, Donald Hamman was saying to his congregation that Medinah Baptist had a great opportunity for growth ahead, but that if the church wanted to grow it had to streamline its decision-making process. It had to get rid of the bulky and cumbersome committee structure. It had to implement the principle underlying this whole chapter: *the pastor has the power in a growing church.*

The congregation bought Hamman's plan and made him company commander. In doing so, they voted out of existence 15 standing committees![5] What has happened since?

The church was growing well when all this took place in 1970, but it has been growing even better ever since. The growth rate for the five years preceeding the "Crossroads Message" was 253% (projected to the decadal rate) and for the five years afterwards it went up to 325%. That figures down to an increase in the average annual rate from 13.4% to 15.6%.

Good progress!

Melodyland and Calvary Chapel

Two other brief case studies reinforce this point that the pastor has the power in a growing church. Consider here the position of the pastor in the two churches in Southern California which attract the largest congregations at Sunday morning worship: Melodyland Christian Center of Anaheim (10,000) and Calvary Chapel at Costa Mesa (8,000).

Melodyland's constitution states that Pastor Ralph Wilkerson "shall be the executive head of the church and the president of the corporation . . . he shall be the spiritual overseer of the church and shall direct all its activities." According to researcher Henry Lord, this policy works out in practice. He says that Wilkerson "is the controlling power in this church . . . he works under the control of the Holy Spirit and so has his authority from God . . . He uses deacons as advisors and for legal purposes. . . ."[6]

In Calvary Chapel, Pastor Chuck Smith is in charge of the church and holds himself accountable directly to the Lord. The constitution says, "The pastor shall be the president of the corporation and have the general supervision of the entire program and shall perform all necessary duties relating to such supervision."

The Rough Road to Leadership

As we have indicated earlier, the process of earning the love and trust of a congregation is far from an automatic one. Often it will bring the pastor who has a vision for growth up against a severe personal crisis experience. I have heard pastor after pastor tell of heart-rending situations where their leadership was challenged and where it took all the courage and faith in God they could possibly muster to weather the storm.

In public I have heard W. A. Criswell of First Baptist Dallas tell of his crisis experience with his board of deacons. I have heard Robert Schuller tell of his desire to die of a heart attack so he could fail with honor when an obstinate consistory stood in the way of the vision God had given him for growth. I have heard several similar stories in private, some too intimate to relate.

Elmer Towns told me of one pastor who broke down in tears when he recalled his leadership crisis experience. Theological seminaries do not usually prepare young people for such crises, and I fear that too many ministers who are faced with them come out on the losing end and limp through the rest of their ministries, bruised and resigned to mediocrity.

This is not to say that a pastor continually at odds with his people will turn out to be a leader for church growth. The crisis experience I am talking about is not a regular pattern. It usually happens only once. As a result, some good members may leave the church disgruntled and bitter. That is regrettable, but it is part of the price that often needs to be paid.

The leader must be the leader. As Robert Schuller has said, "Let there be no dodging of this issue. Pastor? Do you hear me? You should be the spark plug. You should be the inspiring commander leading the troops up the hill!"[7]

Maintain Your Authority

The pastor of a growing church who has earned his authority also knows how to maintain it. He leads. He is out in front. But never too far in front. My own pastor's wife, Anne Ortlund, suggests in her book *Up With Worship* that sometimes the preacher needs to learn more from his people than his people need to learn theology. "Listen to your dear flock," she pleads. "Get to know them deeply, their needs, their joys . . . *Scratch 'em where they itch.*"[8]

It usually turns out that way. The pastor of a growing church may appear to outsiders to be a dictator. But to the people of the church, his decisions are their decisions. Almost as if he had a sixth sense, he knows how to lead the church where the people want to go, and he also knows how to catalyze the people so they themselves enter into the total work of the church enthusiastically and get the job done.

Let's take a look next at how all this happens!

STUDY QUESTIONS

1. What are some of the personal characteristics of pastors with growing churches?

2. How do the people at the church see such a pastor? Do they see him differently than you see your pastor? If so, name some of the differences.

3. How fast should a church grow? How fast does your church grow?

Footnotes

1. *Decision* Magazine Staff, *Great Churches of Today* (Minneapolis: World Wide Publications, 1973).

2. Elmer L. Towns, *America's Fastest Growing Churches* (Nashville: John T. Benson Publishing Company, 1972).

3. Unpublished dissertation, Fuller Theological Seminary, Pasadena, California, 1975. Also disseminated in an article in *Church Growth: America* (Vol. I, No. 2, 1975). Mylander's label "composite membership" seems to have caught on, and I highly recommend its use as a standard instrument in America.

4. Viggo B. Olsen, *Case Study of Medinah Baptist Church*, unpublished manuscript, Wheaton College Graduate School, 1973, p. 6.

5. Donald Hamman's leadership came to the attention of the Christian public through an article by Elmer Towns, "Minister Asks Dismissal of Boards," *Christian Life*, (December, 1970).

6. Henry Lord, *Seven Successful Churches in Southern California*, unpublished dissertation, California Graduate School of Theology, 1975, pp. 119–120.

7. Robert H. Schuller, *Your Church Has Real Possibilities* (Glendale, California: G/L Publications, 1974), p. 53.

8. Anne Ortlund, *Up With Worship* (Glendale, California: G/L Publications, 1975), p. 84.

let's join laymen's lib!

If the first vital sign of a growing church is a pastor who is using his gifts to lead his church into growth, the second is a well-mobilized laity. One cannot function apart from the other any more than blood circulation and respiration can function apart from each other in the human body.

In a smaller church of up to 200 members the pastor can do all the work, and many do. But such a church will not be a *growing* church if he does.

Pastors of growing churches, whether they be large or small, know how to motivate their laypeople, how to create structures which permit them to be active and productive and how to guide them into meaningful avenues of Christian service.

Activating laypeople for church growth has become more feasible in our day than at any other time in recent church history. This is due to what I like to call the "laymen's lib" movement.

The Appearance of Laymen's Lib

Laymen's lib began in the late 1960s with a general awakening throughout American churches of almost all stripes to the biblical teaching on spiritual gifts. As we look back from our present vantage point many of us wonder how it could possibly be that for so many years and even decades God's people had such a low level of both understanding and practice in the area of spiritual gifts. It must have grieved God, as it did the apostle Paul when he wrote to the Corinthians, "Now concerning spiritual gifts, brethern, I would not have you ignorant" (1 Cor. 12:1, *KJV*).

We have been so ignorant, and God has been so patient!

My own opinion is that the Pentecostal movement has played a key role in stimulating laymen's lib. Twenty years ago I studied under one of America's finest evangelical seminary faculties, but when I graduated I had been taught virtually nothing useful concerning spiritual gifts. I was ordained in an evangelical church, but no one asked me what my spiritual gifts were when I was examined by the ordination council. I joined an evangelical mission board that sent me to South America, but neither in the application form nor in the personal interviews was the matter of my spiritual gifts ever raised.

I would consider this almost unbelievable if I were not able to explain it at least to my own satisfaction. I now realize that my seminary professors, the ministers who ordained me and the mission executives were all still struggling to come to comfortable terms with the Pentecostal movement back in the early and mid-1950s. They were still debating whether Pentecostals were true Christians. I recall reading a book on false cults which contained chapters on Christian Science, Mormonism, *Pentecostalism*, Jehovah's Witnesses, and so forth.

Some people were saying that speaking in tongues was produced by the devil himself. Many Christian leaders seemed to be spooked by reports of miraculous healings and prophecies. When the question came up in class in seminary we were usually told to read a book by Benjamin Warfield which argued that many of the biblical gifts were phased out after the church got rolling, and that we were not to look for them in our churches today.

But times have changed. Through the 1960s the charismatic movement began to trickle out of institutional Pentecostalism into many of the denominations that had previously opposed it. The leaders of the large Pentecostal denominations such as Assemblies of God and Church of the Foursquare Gospel developed rapport and then fellowship with their counterparts in other denominations. Pentecostalism gradually became respectable, and one of the many benefits for non-Pentecostals was a more relaxed attitude toward the biblical teaching on spiritual gifts.

By the mid-1960s the matter of spiritual gifts had become one of my own areas of high priority interest. I attempted myself to clarify issues in a book on First Corinthians,[1] but I believe the real turning point to be the publication of *Body Life,* written by Pastor Ray Stedman of Peninsula Bible Church in Palo Alto, California.[2] The unusual popularity of that book in 1972 is due largely to a receptive climate for spiritual gifts that already had been five years in the making.

Laymen's lib had begun in force!

The subject of spiritual gifts has since become one of the hot items in theological seminaries. Recent graduates have been trained to avoid the clericalism of the past, and to consider themselves "enablers" rather than old-fashioned parsons. Many consider their top priority is to get the laypeople of their churches active in the life of their church.

Pastor Lloyd Ogilvie of Hollywood Presbyterian Church says, "We do not allow the people of the church to call those of us on the staff 'ministers.' We want every member of the church to consider himself or herself a minister of God." All these signs indicate that, more than ever before in recent memory, we live in an age where the layperson is a prominent factor in churches everywhere.

"Total Mobilization" Can Go Sour

As far as church growth is concerned, laymen's lib has opened up fantastic new possibilities. If laypeople become excited about what they can do for God and for their church, the sky is the limit. But it is a fact of life that mere increased activity on the part of the laypeople in a church does not always help that church to grow.

Research has shown that some massive, well organized, heavily financed efforts to achieve "total mobilization" of congregations for evangelism has hindered rather than helped church growth. Some of these efforts have reminded me of a boat with a big motor but a defective rudder. It has plenty of power, but fails to arrive at its destination.

It is no longer a mystery why this happens. Increased knowledge of spiritual gifts has identified the defects of unproductive efforts at "total mobilization." During the 1960s, one of the guiding philosophies of evangelism called the "Strachan theorem"—after Kenneth Strachan of the Latin American Mission—suggested that "the expansion of any movement is in direct proportion to its success in mobilizing its total membership in continuous propagation of its beliefs." In nation after nation, denomination after denomination, church after church, this was attempted for at least a decade. But in virtually no case did it succeed in becoming (1) a total mobilization of church members for evangelistic work, (2) a continuous mobilization in cases where the initial enthusiasm was high or, consequently, (3) a contributing factor in helping churches to increase their previous rates of growth.[3]

Why did such efforts fizzle? Certainly not because of advocating the mobilization of laity as a necessary factor for growth. No, the problem arises when everyone is expected to be a "continuous propagator." This is contrary to one of the major biblical teachings on spiritual gifts, namely "If the whole body were an eye, where were the hearing?" (1 Cor. 12:17, *KJV*). If everybody in the church is expected to be an evangelist, where are those with all the other spiritual gifts that are needed to make those with the gift of evangelist most effective?

Are Five Legs Better Than Two?

Think now in terms of the human body. Suppose our goal

for the moment is to walk to a place a long distance away in the shortest period of time. Suppose we had the power to transpose one member of our body into another.

Would it make any sense to say we could walk faster with five legs than with two, so we will thus change our liver, our tongue and one lung to legs? Of course not. With no liver, one hundred legs would not be able to operate at all. God has fashioned our physical bodies in perfect proportion so that all members work in harmony to help each other function as they should.

But this is exactly what the Bible says God has done with the Church, the body of Christ. In each of the three major lists of spiritual gifts in the Bible, Romans 12, 1 Corinthians 12 and Ephesians 4, they are placed in the context of the body of Christ. "God set the members every one of them in the body, as it hath pleased him," (1 Cor. 12:18, *KJV*). Every single believer has been fitted into the body of Christ according to God's master plan, and has been given one or more spiritual gifts to fulfill that function properly.

There is nothing in the Bible to indicate that it is up to Christians to choose their spiritual gifts for themselves. The choice is up to God, and the first responsibility of every Christian is to discover which of the gifts God has given him.

In the process, of course, it is natural that the person will also discover which of the gifts God has *not* given him. *Both* are extremely important. One of the most pathetic things in a church is to see someone trying to exercise a spiritual gift he or she does not have. It usually ends up in utter frustration, like trying to write on a blackboard with your toes.

Discovering Your Spiritual Gift

In light of the doctrine of spiritual gifts, mobilization of church members for church growth—or any other spiritual activity—must begin with whatever process is necessary for every church member to discover his or her spiritual gift. After this, the gifts must be developed and put to full use through appropriate channels and

73

structures. But nothing can be done if believers are not able to think soberly of themselves as Romans 12:3 indicates.

How is this to be done?

It might be helpful simply to list the five steps that are necessary for discovering your spiritual gift:

1. *Explore the possibilities.* Read and study the lists of gifts in the New Testament. Know the options that appear in the Word of God so that you have something rather concrete to look for as you move ahead.

2. *Experiment with as many as possible.* If you do not try a particular gift, you will have a hard time knowing whether you have it or not. Obviously there are some gifts in the list that are hard to know how to experiment with. No one should jump off a tall building to see if he has the gift of miracles, for example. But many of them, including the gift of evangelist, lend themselves to serious experimentation.

3. *Examine your feelings.* If you try a gift out and enjoy doing it, that is a good sign. On the other hand if you find yourself disliking the task the gift involves, that in itself is a fairly good sign that God hasn't given it to you.

4. *Evaluate your effectiveness.* Spiritual gifts are functional. Each one is designed to accomplish some specific objective. If you begin to think you have a certain spiritual gift be sure that you see the appropriate results when you use it. If you get no results, you may not have the gift.

5. *Expect confirmation from the body.* No gifts can be discovered, developed or used alone. Why? Because they are members of a total organism, the body. If you have a spiritual gift, it will fit with others. Other Christians will recognize your gift and confirm to you that you have it. If you think you have a gift, but no one else agrees you have it, be very suspicious of your assessment in the matter.

Once these five steps are taken and surrounded with much prayer, you should be able to answer clearly and concisely when asked: "What is your spiritual gift?"

I myself have found that God has given me three: the gifts

of teacher, administrator and missionary. I try to be very conscientious in using all the time and energy at my disposal in the
development and use of these gifts. After all, when I come up
to the final judgment, God is going to have me give an account
of how I have used these gifts. I must keep in mind also that
He is not going to make me account for using gifts He has never
given me—and that is a comforting thought!

The Gift of Evangelist

It is obvious that the one gift above all others necessary for
church growth is the gift of evangelist. This comes up in the
list in Ephesians 4:11, where we are also told that the purpose
of all the gifts together is the edification of the body of Christ
(see 4:12). For some reason it did not occur to me until recently
that "edification" means more than building the faith of believers,
which is certainly important. It also refers to adding more cells
or members to the body. In other words, it means church growth.

Church growth occurs when the gift of evangelist is being used,
but it will not happen if the other gifts are not operating simultaneously. In the human body, for example, the uterus is an organ
designed primarily for reproduction, but it is ineffective if the
pituitary gland and the small intestine and any number of other
organs are not working as they should at the same time.

It should be self-evident by now, if what we have said about
spiritual gifts is valid, *not every Christian is an evangelist.* Evangelists are those Christians to whom God has given the spiritual
gift of evangelist. No other members of the body are evangelists,
nor should they try to function as evangelists any more than
ears should try to function as fingers. This is one of the main
reasons why some of the efforts at "total mobilization" have ended
up as frustrations and failures and have had negative rather than
positive influences on church growth.

The Role of Witness

Consider now another extremely important concept: Whereas
every Christian is not an *evangelist,* every Christian certainly is

a *witness.* This important technical distinction prevents Christians who have spiritual gifts other than evangelist from copping out of their responsibility to share Christ with others.

In order to understand this more thoroughly, we must be clear on distinguishing between spiritual gifts and Christian roles. Gifts are the special, vocational functions that God expects each Christian to exercise, and they will differ from one another. Roles, on the other hand, are more natural, everyday functions that all Christians are expected to exercise.

In this sense, roles are related to fruit of the spirit as in Galatians 5:22. Love, joy, peace and longsuffering are not gifts given to certain Christians, but fruit that God expects in the life of every Christian regardless of the gift he or she has. As a matter of fact, the Corinthians learned that in spite of the fact that they had an abundance of spiritual gifts, they were ineffective because they did not combine them with the fruit of the Spirit. First Corinthians 13 was written to bring this out.

Many of the spiritual gifts have a corresponding *role.* One of the gifts, for example, is that of liberality (see Rom. 12:8). Those who have that gift give their material resources to God's work in great abundance and enjoy doing it. But the corresponding role is that every Christian should give regularly to God's work (see 1 Cor. 16:2), and in my opinion should give something above ten percent of his or her gross income.

Another example is the gift of faith—the kind that removes mountains (see 1 Cor. 12:9, 13:2). All Christians will not have this gift, but all do have a role of living a life characterized by faith, for "without faith it is impossible to please" God (see Heb. 11:6, *KJV*).

To repeat, then, only a certain number of Christians have the *gift of evangelist,* but every Christian has the *role of witness.* These two, as we shall see, must combine to mobilize the maximum force for evangelism in your church.

The Hypothesis of the Ten Percent

If not all Christians have the gift of evangelist, how many do?

I was asking myself that question when I moved from Bolivia to the U.S.A. in 1971 because I had done enough research by then to know that the Strachan theorem was defective. I decided to take an empirical approach, so I asked the question: has any church pulled it off?

Has any church, *primarily because of the way it mobilized its membership for evangelism,* shown notable increase in church growth? The answer came quickly: The Coral Ridge Presbyterian Church in Fort Lauderdale, Florida is the bright and shining example.

So I researched the church. I have read about it, I have seen it on film, I have visited it, I have talked to its leaders. The church was down to a low water mark of 17 members when Pastor James Kennedy began mobilizing the membership under the program now called Evangelism Explosion. In 12 years it grew to 2,500 members.

The first impression I had of the church was that everybody was in the Evangelism Explosion program, but later I found that it was not so. How many were in it? Only 250, or ten percent of the membership. From this basis I developed a hypothesis which goes like this: *In the average evangelical church, ten percent of the members have been given the gift of evangelist.*

For three years now I have tested this hypothesis time and time again. My graduate students, who are professional pastors and missionaries, have tested it as well. So far, it has proven to be a very realistic and workable rule of thumb, both in the U.S.A. and in other countries in the Third World. There is, of course, somewhat of a biblical basis for this position, although the hypothesis of the ten percent is empirical rather than exegetical.

Still, when Jesus left the earth, He left a nuclear group of about 120 committed believers in the First Church of Jerusalem. Of them, He had carefully selected and trained ten percent—the 12 apostles—for the specific task of propagating the gospel, while the other 108 had the role of being faithful witnesses, and exercised it.

The church grew magnificently!

Some may disagree with the ten percent figure. If so, set your own percentage, higher or lower, but be sure it is (1) realistic and (2) helpful. My studies so far have shown that setting a goal of mobilizing ten percent for the direct work of evangelism is both realistic and helpful.

I recently discussed the matter with Archie Parrish, who has been heading up the Evangelism Explosion program at Coral Ridge Presbyterian. He reported that with a current membership of 3,000, a full 450 were active in the program. The 10% had become 15%.

Wonderful!

I have a hunch, however, that this record is somewhat parallel to a baseball player's batting around .350. Years of experience have shown that if a player can maintain a .280 or .300 average, he is an outstanding hitter. I think that if year in and year out a church can maintain 10% of its membership in active evangelism, it is an outstanding church. Players like Ty Cobb (.367 lifetime) and churches like Coral Ridge are unusual.

As a matter of fact, if a church mobilizes the ten percent who have the gift of evangelist, and if these people win only one convert per year—a poor showing for a person with the gift—and bring that person into church membership, the church will triple every ten years. Or, in more precise terms, the church can plan on a decadal rate of 200%. This is not even faith—it is a matter of simple mathematics. Faith can take the church much farther.

The Problem of the Nine-Point-Five

Why then are not more churches growing at 200% per decade? In my opinion, one of the major obstacles to church growth today is the following: *Of the 10% to whom God has given the gift of evangelist, only about one half of one percent are actively using it.* The other 9.5% have the gift; but some don't know they have it, and some don't even know there is any such thing as spiritual gifts. Also, some may think they have it, but are not afforded good opportunities or proper encouragement to use it well.

A very serious problem arises when the blame is misplaced.

The Strachan theorem type of "total mobilization" tends to lay blame on the 90% who never had the gift of evangelist in the first place. This is counterproductive, since it develops unnecessary guilt complexes in the majority of church members. As a result the church can be full of gloomy and depressed Christians who (1) repel by their very attitude the new converts who are being won, yet who don't want to join a gloomy church and (2) find themselves in no psychological condition to move on and discover the spiritual gifts they do have. There is no way that a church in this condition can expect to grow.

Thus, the focus of attention for mobilizing the basic evangelistic potential of the church should be on the 9.5% of the members who have the gift of evangelist but are not using it. They *should* feel guilty if they are not evangelizing. If the effort is directed here, the first step toward mobilization of spiritual gifts for growth has been taken.

The Mobilization of the Ninety Percent

Many churches have active and productive evangelistic programs, but still a particular church does not grow over the years. People are being converted, baptisms are frequent and new members are coming in all the time. But at the same time, members are drifting away. The front door is wide open, but many who enter it soon find their way out the back door.

What is the problem here?

More often than not, the problem will lie with the 90%. Just because these people don't have the gift of evangelist, they should not be allowed to forget that they do have some spiritual gift that needs to be used. The nurture of the new converts and the process of folding them into the body is equally as important as their conversion as far as church growth is concerned. Here is a crucial function of the pulpit ministry and the Sunday School.

I believe that attending Sunday School should be made almost a requirement for church membership. And I also believe that one of the primary objectives of the Christian education program of the church should be to enable every single person in the church, within one year after conversion in the case of adults or sometime before the 25th birthday of second generation Christians, to come to terms with his or her spiritual gift—to know precisely what it is and to be using it effectively. If this is done, the guilt feelings that might have built up because certain people did not have certain gifts will be removed, and the whole body will be healthy and ready for good growth.

One pastor who has done this successfully is David Libby of Trinity Congregational Church, Bolton, Massachusetts. He accepted the pastorate of a developing rural church in 1968. The church was a remodeled barn, with a sanctuary seating 80 in the front and Sunday School in the back.

After a period of ministry of healing within the body, Libby started planning for growth. He began preaching verse-by-verse expository sermons. Some new people came in, and by the beginning of 1974 the congregation of 30 had grown to 50.

Then all of a sudden, while preparing a sermon one day, he came up short. He was in 1 Peter, and was preparing to preach on the text: "As every man hath received the gift, even so minister the same one to another" (1 Pet. 4:10, *KJV*). He couldn't preach on it!

Why?

On an annual congregational survey the previous New Year, not a single member of the congregation was able to answer the question: "What is your spiritual gift?"

He changed his preaching schedule on the spot. He switched from expository to topical messages and preached 22 consecutive sermons on spiritual gifts! By the twenty-second Sunday both David Libby and his people were on a spiritual gift high.

He passed out a mimeographed questionnaire in the morning service, in order to help people discover gifts they never knew they had before. By the end of 1974 the congregational survey showed that every member but one had come to know what his or her spiritual gift was.

The congregation was mobilized, and ready to move!

Within four months they had to knock the wall out of the

barn. On the first Sunday they went from 80 seats to 160, there was standing room only. Granted, it was Easter Sunday, but the attendance held and the church continues full. Now they have projected building a new sanctuary on their seven acres of farm land. And all this in rural New England!

As soon as I heard this, I asked David Libby how many of the 25 communicant members who filled out the questionnaire had the gift of evangelist. He said that two did, and he himself was not one of them. This brings up an important concept: *The pastor of a growing church does not necessarily need to have the gift of evangelist, although he should be very active in using his role of witness.*

The key function of the pastor, then, is not that he evangelize, but that he lead his people into discovering, developing and using their God-given spiritual gifts.

Utilizing the Role of Witness

Even though it is conceded that the 90% who have gifts other than the gift of evangelist also have a *role of witness,* in some the potential for effective use of this role for church growth is greater than in others. In order to explain this, let me set forth another hypothesis which may sound strange at first: *The effectiveness of the Christian's role as a witness for church growth decreases with that person's maturity in Christ.*

We usually assume that just the opposite is true. We feel that the longer a person is a Christian, the more he knows about the Word of God, the deeper his prayer life, the fewer bad habits he has and, consequently, the better he is equipped for evangelism. But this is not necessarily true.

There are two good reasons for this seemingly strange phenomenon. The first is that older Christians simply have fewer contacts with non-Christians. When a person becomes a Christian he starts a new life, and in most cases that life centers in a new social institution called a church. If healthy Christian growth takes place in his life, the new convert becomes more and more involved in the church.

Many hours of his free time are now spent with other Christians in worship, prayer, Sunday School, committees and church-sponsored social events. He makes new friends, but almost all of his new friends are Christians. If he is a convinced believer, within two or three years all his old friends know he is a Christian. He has witnessed to them, some have accepted Christ, some have decided not to become Christians and there are very few more good prospects for sharing Christ in his circle of friends and acquaintances.

Notice that the same principle applies to most second generation Christians. Sons and daughters of Christian parents, who have been raised in the church, have fairly well limited their circle of friends to Christians, so even when they are converted their potential for evangelism is not very high compared to that of a new convert from the world.

The second reason why older Christians have very little evangelistic potential is the phenomenon called "redemption and lift." The very power of the Christian life that is generated within a new convert may soon lift him out of his former environment. For many, this means social and economic advance. For all, it should mean the development of a different life-style which the Bible calls "separation from the world." But as this process develops, a gap between the Christian and his unsaved friends opens wider and wider, until in some cases very little can be shared with them on a deeper personal level.

This does not mean that any Christian with the role of witness may be negligent when opportunities come to lead others to Christ. All Christians at all times should be prepared for that moment when God brings them into contact with a person prepared by the Holy Spirit for accepting Christ. And they should know how to introduce that person to Christ. Here is where an ingenious device like the *Four Spiritual Laws* is an invaluable tool, and the more Christians who know how to use such a tool in conjunction with their role of witness, the better.[4]

What all this means is that *you do not build a total strategy for evangelism and church growth on this kind of occasional contact*

on the part of older Christians. The highest potential for evangelism
through the role of witness comes from new converts who still have
many natural bridges to unsaved friends and relatives. If your church
runs out of new converts, its evangelistic potential drops sharply.

Putting It All Together

What is the conclusion of all that has been said? Simply this:
The greatest potential for evangelistic effectiveness in a church comes
from a combination of the 10% of the mature Christians who have
the gift of evangelist with those recent converts of less than three
years in the Lord in a program planned and designed for church
growth. Put this together with the 90% who know and are using
their other spiritual gifts, and you have developed the kind of
mobilization that produces an extremely high growth potential.

STUDY QUESTIONS

1. What are some of the activities that you see an enabling
pastor doing?

2. Do you know what your spiritual gift or gifts are? Have
you taken the steps that the author recommends?

3. How many people in your church have the gift of evangelism?
Name them. What percentage of the church do they represent?

Footnotes

1. C. Peter Wagner, *A Turned-on Church in an Uptight World* (Grand Rapids: Zondervan Publishing House, 1971).
2. Ray C. Stedman, *Body Life* (Glendale, California: G/L Publications, 1972).
3. I have documented some of this research on "total mobilization" in my book, *Frontiers in Missionary Strategy* (Chicago: Moody Press, 1972), and additional evidence on the subject has been published elsewhere.
4. *Four Spiritual Laws* (Arrowhead Springs, California: Campus Crusade for Christ).

how big
is big enough?

The third vital sign characteristic of growing churches in America is that they are big enough. By "big enough" I do not want to suggest any magic number of members for optimum size, nor do I want to give the impression that I am a superchurch addict. I thank God for some of the big churches and I thank God for some of the smaller churches. But at the same time, I am embarrassed by some of the big churches, just as I am embarrassed by some of the smaller churches.

A few months ago, for example, the *Los Angeles Times* ran a major article on the front page under the headline: "Superchurches of Radio, T.V. in Financial Bind; Naive and Sometimes Misguided Leadership by Clergymen is Blamed."[1] Those of us in the family of God know very well that names mentioned in that article such as Rex Humbard, Jerry Falwell and Charles Blair are warmhearted, dedicated servants of God who are intent on using their spiritual gifts to the maximum in winning Americans to Christ for the glory of God. They are not scoundrels or wolves in sheep's clothing, although I suppose that most non-Christians who read the *Los Angeles Times* would have received that impression. That's what I mean by some churches being embarrassing. None of us likes our family's dirty laundry to be hung out in public.

Such publicity may also be misleading, which is even more dangerous. When some Christians hear that certain superchurches have made embarrassing mistakes they are likely to conclude that all big churches are bad. This is not a reasonable generalization.

In urban areas where 74% of Americans live, growing churches have become large enough to provide the variety and quality of services that members have come to expect from a modern church. This is really a fairly simple sociological principle. In our American society, with the exception of certain rural communities and among certain ethnic groups, the church is a voluntary association.

If a church meets people's needs they will become members. When it no longer meets their needs they will either drop out altogether or change churches. The more secularized a society becomes, the less inherent social pressure keeps forcing people to belong to a church, no matter what. As we all know, our American society is highly secularized and becoming more so. If churches do not match up to the people's expectations they simply cannot grow.

Big Churches vs. Small Churches

First of all, I wish to disassociate myself from the big-church-small-church debate. The reason for this is that small churches are big enough to meet some people's needs, but other people require large churches to meet their needs.

Some people will always feel more secure in a small church. They need to sense that they are an intimate part of the whole social unit. They feel uncomfortable when they look around and see a large number of strange faces.

They also like to feel that they are needed, and thus are adverse to entering into the heavy competition for leadership that comes with a large church. They want to be missed when they are absent and they like to believe that the church wouldn't be quite the same without their membership. Obviously, a small church best meets the needs of this kind of person.

Others have a very different makeup. They need to feel that

they are where the action is. They enjoy seeing piled-up traffic and long lines of Sunday School buses around their church on Sunday mornings. Posters and banners are attractive to them.

Many members of large churches appreciate the opportunity to be rather anonymous when they go to church. They don't like fusses made over them or their families. They prefer to be in a crowd where they can choose their own friends rather than having certain friends forced upon them. This kind of person naturally needs a large church.

Consequently, as I see it, we will have a continuing need in America for both big churches and small churches in the foreseeable future. But whether a church is large or small, *it should be a growing church*. It should be adding to its number "daily such as should be saved" (Act 2:47, *KJV*). As long as there are unsaved people in its community, a church cannot be content with the status quo. Healthy large churches and healthy small churches are evangelistically effective.

Notice the implications of the above reasoning, however:

1. If smaller churches are growing they eventually will become large churches. Just as every river was once a stream, every large church was once a small church. When this happens, new small churches will continually be needed.

2. Percentage-wise, the larger a church is the more people it will win to Christ, provided the same rate of conversion growth is maintained—and admittedly this is not easy to do.

Advantages of Large Churches

Generally speaking, pastors of large churches have come to feel that they can get the job of evangelism and Christian nurture done better than pastors of small churches can. All one has to do is to make the circuit of the seminars mentioned earlier and listen to the testimonies of the pastors who hold them.

One obvious advantage they have is that—almost without exception—pastors of large churches have at one time or another also been pastors of small churches. They have seen both sides of the coin. They have a personal point of comparison.

86

The opposite, however, is rarely true—very few pastors of small churches have ever been pastors of large churches. I suppose this helps explain why church growth people generally listen well when the pastor of a large church tells how he does it.

Up to a point, I can empathize with the impatience that pastors of large churches have with much of the criticism that is leveled against them. I am not a pastor, but my own Lake Avenue Congregational Church has 3,000 members and falls into the large church category. When I mention this, I often get the response: "Oh, that's too big!"

But I have learned to reply: "Too big for what?" The answer to that one is hard to come by.

Our church is not too big to provide a first-rate pulpit ministry. It's not too big to put together a professionally executed worship service that brings believers into soul-stirring contact with God every Sunday morning. It's not too big to provide a vital youth program geared to the special needs of each age group. It's not too big to provide expert pastoral counseling.

It's not too big to offer opportunities for close friendships, more casual acquaintances, vital community involvement, sound biblical teaching, openings for Christian service of all kinds, a missionary program that makes a difference in world evangelization, the finest in sacred music, and . . . I could go on and on.

The basic reason a large church can provide these services is that it can afford to hire a well-trained and experienced staff. Running a modern church in America is a professional job. The very existence of theological seminaries verifies this fact. They are designed as clearly for professional training as medical schools are in their field.

Notice also that larger churches not only can hire more people who are specialists in one field or another, but they can also afford to pay them enough to keep them. It may not seem spiritual, but there is a discernible relationship between salary scales and ministerial longevity. And, it is a fact that churches which keep pastors longer are more likely to grow. Pastors are people too, and if they are comfortable they are less likely to be looking around for greener pastures.

Except for providing a familiar environment for those people who feel insecure with excitement and strangers, a large church can do just about everything a small church can do, but not vice versa. A church can be *too small* for lots of things. I think, for example, that our church, at 3,000 members, may be too small for a highly effective singles ministry. I began to suspect this when I heard Robert Schuller say that their singles program limped along until their church passed the 5,000 membership mark. When they were over 5,000 they had enough single adults in each age bracket to grade the program properly—and then it soared.

Speaking of Robert Schuller, consider how he presents the big church vs. small church matter to potential converts. His church subscribes to the Telecredit service which gives him a printout of all the closings on residential property purchases in his area. His staff sends out 27,000 form letters per year to new families in the neighborhood.

On the very first page of the form letter, a sub-title appears: "The Smallest Church and the Biggest Church in Orange County." In it he says, "While over 7,000 people attend the five services every Sunday, we have it structured in such a way that people who like small churches can attend the little Chapel-in-the-Sky at the top of the Tower where they have a view from the Santa Ana mountains to Catalina Island floating in the ocean beyond the coast line."

Everyone knows, of course, that this is a come-on. It is designed to get them to go to the "small church" and in the process try the "big church" as well. It's the "try it, you'll like it" approach.

The fact of the matter is that if only 3% of the members of Garden Grove attended the Chapel-in-the-Sky, there would be standing room only every Sunday. It seats only 200. But many who try it like it, as Garden Grove's sustained growth rate of 500% per decade indicates.

Bigness as an Evangelistic Tool

The attraction of a complete church program designed to meet all kinds of human needs can be a powerful evangelistic tool. Few know how to exploit this potential as well as does Robert Schuller. He does it big once a year—on Easter Sunday. On the theory that more unchurched people are willing to listen to the claims of Christ on Easter than any other day of the year, the Garden Grove Community Church pulls out all the stops on that day.

Garden Grove's Easter Sunday church bulletin this past Easter was more than a bulletin, it was a sixteen-page, tabloid-sized advertising extravaganza. What does it advertise? All the services that Garden Grove Church offers to meet a wide variety of needs of the people in Orange County. It reproduces articles on the church from *Time, Christian Life,* and *Los Angeles Times* to let people know that they have come to a place where some notable action is occuring.

The bulletin tells them about personalized pastoral counseling so people will not think church members are just a computer number. It advertises Sunday School and Bible teaching programs for children, young people and adults. It offers the various singles programs. And it tells them of opportunities for backpacking, camping, sports, boating and other activities for youth.

The bulletin goes on to describe musical programs in no less than sixteen choirs. It invites women to candlelight dinners and a luncheon with Mrs. Jack LaLanne. It lets them know about the Hour of Power television ministry nationwide. And the center spread splashes out the architect's drawing of their planned 4,000 seat sanctuary.

One of the objectives of this massive promotional effort is to get the unchurched Easter visitor back the following Sunday. At that time Schuller delivers "The Greatest Sermon Ever Preached," a completely choreographed recitation of Jesus' Sermon on the Mount, and which has to qualify as one of the most spectacular pulpit presentations in contemporary Christendom. From there the inquirers are enrolled in the pastor's class where evangelist

Calvin Rynbrandt seeks to lead them to a personal relationship with Jesus Christ and then into church membership.

How About the Smaller Churches?

I realize that it is not easy for everyone to identify with a superchurch like Garden Grove. Even when we remember that there was a time not too long ago when Garden Grove had 50 members, 100 members, 350 members and so forth, not many people in America are where it is now.

According to Lyle Schaller's research, a full 95% of the churches in America average under 350 for Sunday morning worship. Half the churches in the country have 75 or less out on Sunday morning. This means that if you have 100 out on Sunday morning you are well above average, and if you have 400, you are a big church by comparative standards.

But the chances are that your church, whatever the membership, is not big enough. The chances are that you would do well to put church growth principles into practice and trust God for a 100% or 200% increase over the next ten years.

An enlightening piece of research was done recently by Willys Braun in connection with a church growth project in the Christian and Missionary Alliance, a denomination of relatively small churches. It shows that even among small churches, the slightly larger ones seem to be more suited for effective evangelism than the slightly smaller ones.

During "Operation Harvest" in 1972 it was found that C&MA churches which had memberships ranging from 150-200 members produced the greatest percentage of converts. Churches that size are the biggies in the Alliance, with only 4% of Alliance churches that large. But those 4% of the churches produced a full 31% of the total denominational growth!

Braun's rather startling observation was stated like this: "We could have had the same growth if by some sort of National League trade arrangement we had exchanged 1,147 of our other churches for 193 more of this size!"

More directly, Braun questioned the value of budgeting denominational funds for churches in the 1-25 membership category, when the investment of the same funds in the churches of the 125-150 category, to help them move to the 150-200 level, would undoubtedly result in accelerated church growth for the denomination as a whole. For the Alliance, evidently, 125 members in a church is not big enough.

Braun didn't raise the question, but I wonder how a half dozen Alliance churches of 500-600 members would compare to the rest? Possibly the top 4% would do even better if they were bigger.

The Optimum Growth Factor

This brings us to the next question: How big is big enough? Suppose you do move into a pattern of growth—is there any optimum growth level you should aim for?

The optimum growth factor is not a frequent topic of discussion in the writings of pastors of superchurches. One does not find Jerry Falwell or W. A. Criswell or James Kennedy setting limits on their growth. This is understandable since exercising leadership in large, growing churches is part and parcel of the very life-style of these pastors.

Schuller says: "One thing is certain: a church must never stop growing. When it ceases to grow it will start to die."

But I feel there may be a danger here. Postulating unlimited expansion growth can turn out to be deceptive and ultimately counterproductive. There must be a limit to the growth of a local congregation somewhere.

The largest church membership I have come across is the Jotabeche Methodist Pentecostal Church of Santiago, Chile, with 80,000. The largest sanctuary I am aware of is the 25,000-seat Brazil for Christ church in Sao Paulo, Brazil. Both of these churches, however, are structured around what Donald MacNair calls the "satellite" principle, a cluster of semi-autonomous daughter congregations which relate in a dynamic way to the mother church and to each other.

I doubt very much if we are going to see a local church with a composite membership of, say, 25,000 in America—although

I would be glad to be proved wrong. But plot the graphs of growth of the larger churches on a semi-logarithmic graph, and almost invariably the curve flattens out as the church gets larger. And use that composite membership figure to keep everyone honest. Certainly church growth planning should take this matter of optimum growth more seriously than has been done to date.

By raising the issue of optimum growth, I do not want to be forced to set certain numbers as a limit. David Mains discussed limits in his book *Full Circle*[2] and set 200 as the optimum level for Circle Church, Chicago. And in *Christianity Today*,[3] James Davey argued that an ideal optimum size for a church in America is one of 400-600 members.

The Philosophy of Ministry

But rather than dealing with specific figures myself, however, I would like to attempt to articulate some principles. And the first one is this: *The optimum size of each church depends primarily on its philosophy of ministry.*

Churches, much like people, have personalities that set them apart one from another. Some of their personalities are rather undesirable, and thus they do not attract many new members.

But others, particularly the growing churches, have developed fascinating personalities. They have characteristics that to one degree or another give the church a self-identity that makes it unique.

Park Street Church of Boston, Mariners Church of Newport Beach (California), Calvary Temple of Denver and Bel Air Presbyterian of Los Angeles, for example, are all magnificent churches—but vastly different from one another. For underlying each church personality is a distinct philosophy of ministry.

Just as every Christian has a spiritual gift, every church has a philosophy of ministry. Some know what it is and can articulate it; some don't even know there is any such thing.

Unlike spiritual gifts, however, some philosophies of ministry are good and some are not so good. But the first thing a church needs to know before it can come to terms with its optimum growth factor is its philosophy of ministry.

The philosophy of ministry of Lake Avenue Congregational Church, for example, is based on three specific priorities. Circle Church's philosophy of ministry is described by them as the "open church" concept which is heavy on mixing people of differing ethnic backgrounds. Peninsula Bible Church in Palo Alto, California, calls their philosophy of ministry "body life." The Church of the Redeemer in Houston has built a philosophy of ministry around the concept of charismatic Christian community.

There are many good philosophies of ministry and each one will tend to determine certain levels of optimum growth.

Minimum Optimum Growth

What is the guiding principle for determining a level *of minimum optimum growth?* Simply this—a church is not large enough if it cannot yet meet two requirements:

1. It must be large enough for the efficient functioning of its own philosophy of ministry.

2. It must be large enough to provide an adequate base for extension growth.

Part of the technical terminology of church growth is the fourfold classification of *internal growth, expansion growth, extension growth* and *bridging growth:*

Internal growth includes all that happens within the body of Christ among believers. Worship, Christian nurture, counseling, revival or anything that makes Christians better servants of God is internal growth.

Expansion growth occurs when believers move out into the world, win people to Christ and bring them into church membership in their own local congregation. It results in membership growth of the local assembly.

Extension growth means winning people to Christ, but instead of bringing them into the same local church, they are gathered into new churches. It is also called church planting, and new congregations result.

93

Bridging growth also means planting new churches, but in cultures different from the culture of the base church. The cross-cultural aspect makes it a more complex process than extension growth.

In these terms, then, there is obviously no optimum growth limit on extension and bridging growth as long as there are people in the world who have yet to become Christians. With 2.7 billion people in Asia, Africa and Latin America who have not yet heard of Jesus Christ, and with over 100 million unchurched people right here in the United States, there is no way a concerned Christian can talk about optimum *extension* or *bridging* growth.

The Need for Extension Growth

As a matter of fact, I do not hear nearly enough talk about extension growth here in our country. Very few of the churches cited so far have incorporated as a specific part of their regular planning and budget a program to plant new churches. Some have younger offspring and they love them very much, but more often than not they were the result of *accidental* parenthood, not *planned parenthood.*

I have been greatly disappointed to find such a low level of concern for church planting on the part of American pastors. I doubt that a single theological seminary offers a course on how to plant a new church.

It is only natural that when a church does begin to reproduce offspring that these offspring develop a philosophy of ministry similar to that of the mother church. Thus, the number of people necessary for minimum optimum growth will vary according to the philosophy of ministry of the mother church.

Circle Church is realistic in setting a figure of 200 as their minimum optimum growth level. Another church might say 1200. I am ashamed to say that Lake Avenue Church is not yet at its minimum optimum level with 3,000 members. Ashamed, be-cause as yet we have not developed a workable program for planting new churches with our philosophy of ministry, although we hope to do so in the near future.

The best model I have found for a practical application of the optimum growth principle is Redwood Chapel of Castro Valley, California. Pastor Sherman Williams' philosophy of ministry involves a strong emphasis on the development of small, professional-quality musical groups and a television ministry. Integral to their church program also is the planting of a new church with their philosophy of ministry every two years. Their minimum optimum level is around 900.

Maximum Optimum Growth

Facilities always have a good deal to do with determining the *maximum optimum growth level*. A growing church which has arrived at its minimum optimum level will eventually need to face the decision of whether to expand facilities, and if so how much. In most cases, what your church hopes to accomplish on Sunday morning will provide a reasonable criterion for future planning. And this again comes back to the church's philosophy of ministry.

Robert Schuller's main objective on Sunday morning is to impress unchurched people in Orange County. He lives in an area of super shopping centers, Disneyland, Knott's Berry Farm, Anaheim Stadium and the Anaheim Convention Center. Unchurched people there are oriented to the big, the spectacular and the exciting.

Schuller has already outgrown his 1,700-seat sanctuary and 1,500 automobile drive-in parking lot. He is faithful to his philosophy of ministry when he projects a new 4,100-seat sanctuary and a further expansion of what he claims will be the "largest paved church parking lot in the world."

But a similar program would not fit into the philosophy of ministry of Lake Avenue Congregational Church. Pastor Ray Ortlund's objective on Sunday morning is not so much to impress the unchurched as it is to develop a worship experience that brings Christians into the very presence of God. He and his staff have established a whole theology of worship which by general consensus is one of the primary factors contributing to the growth of that church. This kind of worship can best be accomplished in a sanctuary of not more than 2,500. So the maximum optimum growth for Lake Avenue Church would be somewhat less than for Garden Grove Community.

But there is nothing magic about these numbers. A smaller maximum around 350 is realistic for Circle Church and 900 is considered both minimum and maximum for Redwood Chapel. Since their sanctuary doubles as a television studio, Redwood Chapel's present seating capacity of 650 is considered ideal, and Pastor Williams intends to keep to two Sunday morning worship services. Surplus people are used to plant new churches.

In summary, *a growing church can consider itself big enough when it is effectively winning lost people to Christ, when it provides the range of services that meet the needs of its members, and when it is reproducing itself by planting new churches.*

STUDY QUESTIONS

1. What are some of the advantages of a large church? How does your church relate in size? Do you feel the emphasis quoted by the author of Robert Schuller's Garden Grove Community Church on Easter is a practical one for you?

2. What do you think about the author's recommendation as to optimum size of a church? What is your church growth philosophy? Has it been clearly stated? Are you following a specific plan towards a set goal membership and/or average attendance?

3. Has your church ever had a "daughter" church? Are you even pregnant with one? Do you have any intention of ever having offspring?

Footnotes

1. Russ Chandler, "Superchurches of Radio, T.V. in Financial Bind; Naive and Sometimes Misguided Leadership by Clergymen Is Blamed," *Los Angeles Times*, December 1, 1974.
2. David Mains, *Full Circle* (Waco: Word, Inc., 1971).
3. James Davey, *Christianity Today*, November 5, 1971.

celebration +
congregation +
cell = church

The fourth vital sign of a healthy, growing church can be best expressed by this simple formula:

   Celebration + Congregation + Cell = Church.

What does this mathematical expression mean? Let's take it apart and consider it one element at a time, beginning with the first: celebration.

Celebration

One of the things a large church can do well is to celebrate. By "celebrate," I mean roughly what most people mean by "worship," but not entirely. A person can worship God beside a babbling brook in a forest or in his car on a freeway or with his family around the dinner table.

However, none of these situations is conducive to what I mean by celebration. The occasion for that in most churches is on Sunday morning. When a lot of people come together, hungry to meet God, a *special* kind of worship experience can occur. That experience is what I want to call "celebration."

While the relationship is not a direct proportion, size has something to do with the quality of a celebration. As every sports fan knows there is something about a game played before 75,000 spectators that makes it superior to the same game before 1,500.

As every sociologist knows, certain laws of collective behavior operate differently in small groups than in large groups. As every psychologist knows, mob psychology has certain effects on people's emotions and their reactions to stimuli which would not be the case at all if the person were alone or in a small group.

Worship as a Festival

God's people have known about celebration for a long time. The fact that the Temple was the focal point for the worship of Jehovah helped immensely in keeping the twelve tribes of Israel and their respective clans together as the people of God. The temple was so designed that lots of people would be there at one time seeking God and seeing others do the same thing.

By divine appointment not only was there a weekly Sabbath, but great yearly festivals such as the Passover, Pentecost, Day of Atonement, the Feast of Tabernacles, and later Purim and others. Something good happened to God's people during those celebrations that would not have happened without them.

Christian festivals and celebrations have been a longstanding tradition in American Christianity, too, although they have taken on different forms and names at different times. The great camp meetings of a century ago, Finney's revivals, Billy Graham crusades, summer Bible conferences, Urbana missionary conventions—all these have operated basically as celebrations. They were and still are functional substitutes for the Jewish festivals. Christians love to go to them. They are a lot of fun!

Some Sunday morning worship services in our churches are fun, too. Unfortunately, however, in a large number of our churches, the Sunday morning service is more like a funeral than a festival. There is nothing unauthentic about that kind of worship service—true, committed Christians can and do get through to God under such circumstances. But it is not the kind of experience that they are very enthusiastic in inviting their unconverted friends to. Why not admit it? It's no fun!

This is probably one reason why many churches have remained small over the years. Most of them, especially when a new pastor has arrived, have tried to beef up their worship service from time to time so it would be more attractive to outsiders. But in many cases nothing seems to work. The problem could very well be that the churches are simply too small. Good celebrations need lots of people to make them fun and attractive.

Of all the pastors I have associated with, Raymond Ortlund, my own pastor, has most thoroughly grappled with the theology and practice of worship. He says, "Worship is top priority. Everything, absolutely everything, must be put aside to do this thing that God has called you to do. Worship is lofty business—but friend, we do it so poorly."

Ortlund knows that good worship does not just happen. It has to be planned and worked on. So he gives a great deal of his energy to the Sunday morning worship at Lake Avenue Church. And one of his key staff people, Bruce Leafblad, has been called by the church virtually to do only one thing: see that Lake Avenue Church has an exciting celebration at 8:15, 9:30 and 11:00 every Sunday morning.

Leafblad is a pro. He has what many churches need: a spiritual gift for designing recipes that combine choirs and Scripture and preaching and announcements and organ music and offerings and prayer and solos and standing and sitting and noise and silence in such a way that 52 times a year 2,500 people go home to Sunday dinner feeling that they have just had an important meeting with almighty God and that because of it they are not the same.

"Playing Church"

Worship, of course, can never be a one-way street. With all the skill in the world on the platform and in the pulpit, a person in the pew will not meet God if he or she doesn't put anything into it. Christian people have to be motivated and trained to worship well or they will end up "playing church." In our church we are told from the pulpit to avoid playing church with the same finality that we are told to avoid cheating, stealing or adultery. Ray Ortlund's wife, Anne, has learned these lessons so well over the years that she has just written a book on it.[1]

This is not at all to say that Lake Avenue Church has the best or the *only* kind of celebration that will help a church to grow. We do know that it is good for our people in our community at this particular point of history, and we wouldn't trade it for anything. Yet I have seen dozens of other equally effective patterns of celebration so different from my own church's that a person from Mars might wonder if it was the same religion. But if these celebrations bring people to God in such a way that they say to their unchurched friends, "Hey, how about coming to church with me—you'll have a great time!" they will help the church grow.

Congregation

I know when I find a growing church, I will also find a well-executed celebration. However, a good celebration alone does not make for a healthy, growing church. The celebration will generally be there, but it will also be properly balanced with the other two major functions of a local church: congregation and cell.

Celebration + congregation + cell = church. Most churches do not choose one or two of these elements, they combine all three.

The distinction between the celebration and the congregation is a crucial one. Some avoid a celebration because they feel that if they encourage too many people to gather together on a Sunday morning they will lose the sense of personal fellowship, which they value very highly. They are concerned that a Christian in a large celebration might be anonymous. They even feel that fellowship and worship must be so closely related that they plan church seating in a circle rather than in rows. They want eye contact with each other rather than with those on the platform.

Eye contact and fellowship are all necessary, but in the congregation and cell, *not* in the celebration. Anonymity in a celebration is not bad at all. The fact that I am not acquainted with the persons in front of me or behind me in Dodger Stadium, for example, has no effect on my personal involvement in the game.

The same thing applies when I go to church to worship God on Sunday morning. I don't go there to widen my circle of friends or discuss and dialogue. My goal is to meet God, and that ultimately involves just God and me. Anne Ortlund believes so strongly in this that she titled one of the chapters of her book "Three Cheers for Stiff, Rigid Rows of Pews!" Well said!

However, if all a church has to offer is celebration, it may well not be a church. Kathryn Kuhlman's monthly Sunday afternoon meetings in Los Angeles' Shrine Auditorium are great celebrations. Billy Graham rallies are great celebrations. Bill Gothard seminars produce a slightly different form of celebration. But none of these in itself could become a church, precisely because the participants—by the nature of the gatherings—maintain anonymity.

In the congregation the anonymity is lost. If a believer misses two or three celebrations in a row, no one is the wiser. But if he misses two or three meetings of the "congregation," he is worried over, called upon, prayed for and made to understand that there are people around him that care. Deep down, everyone needs to have others know his or her name and use it. The congregation is the place where people know each other's names.

Congregation as a Fellowship Circle

I think I first latched onto the term "congregation" when I read Larry Richard's book, *A New Face for the Church.*[2] He uses "congregation" in relationship to the word "cell," and I like the terminology. Lyle Schaller, who is more sociologically oriented, calls it a "fellowship circle," in contrast to the whole church which he calls the "membership circle." I like this terminology also, although Schaller's "fellowship circle" includes both of what I join Larry Richards in calling the congregation *and* the cell.

The major characteristic of the congregation, as I see it, is that everyone in the congregation is supposed to know everyone else. Here is where fellowship starts, although it does not end here. In smaller churches, of course, the fellowship group and the membership group are likely to be one and the same. In a church of 100 or 200 members you are supposed to recognize a stranger if he wanders in on Sunday morning, and you expect to be missed if for some reason you don't attend.

But not so in a larger church. The congregations there take forms other than that of the membership group. Undoubtedly the most common form of a congregation within a larger church is the Sunday School class. But it can take other forms as well. It can be structured as a neighborhood group which meets regularly. It can be a charismatic prayer meeting. It can be a task-oriented group such as the choir or the evangelism team, or the bus ministry leaders or the commission on social involvement. It can be activity-oriented such as a softball team or a camping club. In many ways—except for celebration, these several congregations within the larger church function exactly like a small country church would be expected to function.

Churches can grow for a time with just a great celebration. But such growth can be illusory. This is one reason for using composite membership figures whenever possible. They balance off Sunday morning attendance and church membership rolls against involvement in congregations, most readily measured by Sunday School attendance.

New York vs. Dallas

Pastor Harold Fickett applied the principle of balancing the celebration with the congregation rigorously as he led the Van Nuys, California, First Baptist Church from a membership of 3,700 to 12,000 in his pastorate of 16 years—a decadal rate of 109%. He learned it from comparing the histories of First Baptist, New York City with First Baptist, Dallas.[3]

The First Baptist Church of New York was one of the great Christian centers of the nation around the turn of the century. I. M. Haldemann was an outstanding man of God and such an exciting preacher that people would line up for blocks just to get a seat at one of his services. The celebration was superb, the church grew, and it is still fondly remembered as a powerful lighthouse for the gospel. But when Haldemann left, decline set in, and now First Baptist is only a shadow of what it once was.

At around the same time, Pastor George Truett was developing a similarly influential church in First Baptist, Dallas. He matched Haldemann's pulpit ability and served his church for 40 years. Many people thought that when Truett left, the church would decline. But it did not. The church continued strong when he left 25 years ago, and it has become even stronger under the new pastor, W. A. Criswell.

As Harold Fickett sees it, the major difference between the two churches was the strong Christian education program developed in Dallas. By the time Truett left, his staff had built the largest Sunday School in the South. In other words, both churches had a wonderful celebration, but the one that ultimately survived combined *celebration* with *congregation.*

Every time I visit Fickett's former church in Van Nuys, I am impressed by how a church of 12,000 members has developed such an effective network of congregations among its membership. With all its size and flamboyancy, members feel as loved and wanted as if they were members of a tiny church in the New England hills.

The Jolly Sixties, for example, gathers some 800 senior citizens into a congregation. Several other congregations have been formed among 500 single-parent families, which makes good sense in the San Fernando Valley where the percentage of single adults in the general population is one of the highest in the nation. Another congregation brings together young married people and still another young married people with children.

Decentralizing Big Churches

While it is true that almost every growing church has developed congregations or fellowship groups within the total church, I feel that in many cases they can be strengthened even more by a careful process of decentralization. If properly decentralized, they can contribute to church growth in a much more powerful way. This decentralization takes two forms: (1) multiplication of congregations and (2) a higher degree of self-government.

Some years ago a fascinating experiment was run by Richard

Myers, a sociologist of religion from Indiana.[4] He divided a number of ministers into two groups. The first group agreed that whenever a Sunday School teacher resigned, he would combine that class with another similar class. The second group agreed that in every department a new teacher would be added and given a new class formed from the existing classes in the department. In other words, the first group reduced the total number of classes and the second group increased the total number of classes. At the end of a year they were to report the results.

What happened?

In the first group, every combined class had decreased in size until it was no larger than either of the two classes that had joined together. In the second group, every class had grown to the size of the other classes before dividing.

This helps confirm what I have long suspected: *If a church makes the multiplication of congregations or fellowship groups a definite part of its planning for growth, the church will almost invariably grow faster.*

How Large Is a Congregation?

What is the optimum size for a congregation? This needs to be discussed, lest some groupings be considered congregations which aren't congregations at all. The largest Sunday School class I ever attended was Jack Hyles' Pastor's Class which preceded the morning worship service in First Baptist, Hammond, Indiana. I suppose there were around 1,500 adults in the class which met in the sanctuary. This group is clearly too big to be considered a congregation or a fellowship group. First Baptist does have congregations, of course, but this should not be counted as one of them.

Just as in the case of the optimum growth of the church as a whole, the *minimum optimum growth* of a congregation will first be determined by its secondary purpose—the primary being fellowship. A softball team of 25 is plenty big enough. But 25 would be far too small for a fellowship group of single adults.

The *maximum optimum growth* of a congregation is limited

by its primary objective of fellowship. Larry Richards pretty well hits the nail on the head when he suggests 250 as the maximum size. Most people are stretched beyond their capacity to be able to relate to 250 others on a first and last name basis with contacts as infrequent as five or six times a month.

For most, 250 will be too many. This suggests that if your church has congregations that have grown to 250, or in many cases even fewer, it might be time to think of dividing them. If you do, it will probably help your church grow.

Self-Government Is Needed

Multiplication of congregations or fellowship groups is the first aspect of decentralization. The second involves a greater degree of self-government in the congregations themselves.

The suggestion of congregational self-government may be a hard one for churches with an Episcopal or Presbyterian form of government to accept. And it may be rather difficult also for many churches with congregational forms of government to accept. Nevertheless, latent energy for growth within a church will be released if each congregation of adults in the church gains a high measure of self-determination.

I came to this realization myself when studying the growth figures of my own congregation, the Mariners Class in Lake Avenue Church. While our church as a whole is growing and our Sunday School is growing, our class of young grandparents' age declined 43% over the past five years. The class has about 125 active members, so it has not reached maximum size.

The Bible teaching is first rate. The class members are warm and friendly and happy. The spiritual tone is high. The physical setting is ideal. But something is wrong or we wouldn't be declining like we have been.

My hunch is that some aspect of our church *structure* is at fault. The first clue of this came when I began to inquire about who is directly responsible for the growth or decline of the Mariners Class. Since it was decline in this case rather than growth, I found the answer rather elusive.

Some said the pastoral staff had the responsibility, some said the Christian Education Committee and some said the Executive Committee of the Mariners Class. Significantly, no one suggested that it might be the class itself. Why? Because the class is so structured that the membership is responsible for no major decision involving its own activities. All major decisions affecting the class are passed down from somewhere above.

When I realized this, I had to ask: What happened to old-fashioned congregationalism? Congregational churches like ours were founded in colonial New England on the principle that every adult member ought to have an active voice in his or her church affairs. This principle works well as long as the church has not passed the maximum size for a true congregation—or 250 members as we have suggested.

But when it gets to 3,000 like ours, the church has long since ceased being a congregation. This is undoubtedly one of the reasons why we consistently have difficulty in gathering even a minimum quorum for a church business meeting. Everyone knows that it is impossible for a huge business meeting to make really crucial decisions, so they stay home when one is called.

The question then becomes: How can large congregational churches maintain the strengths of congregationalism? The answer is both obvious and significant: *Multiply adult congregations within the church and let each enjoy a congregational form of government.*

I would like to see our Mariners Class become Mariners Congregation. We should have our own deacons and name our appropriate committees. Even more, I think we should be able to call our own pastor, who would of course be added to the pastoral staff of the church as a whole. I believe we could raise our own budget to pay the pastor and our other congregational expenses without subtracting a dime from what we already give to the general church budget. Men and women our age are at the stage of life where we need some new challenges or we begin to vegetate. And we have bushels of spiritual energy in our congregation now going to waste.

How well does this description fit other churches? I don't know,

106

but I suspect there are many others like ours. I suspect also that there are ways these ideas can be worked into churches which do not have congregational forms of government.

Notice how some of the other principles already mentioned fit in. Since the pastor is the number one key to growth, our congregation should have one if we expect to grow. This is not intended to detract one bit from the role of the senior pastor without whom it could never happen well.

The laypeople who have not been drawn into the fairly exclusive leadership level of the church as a whole would have a new opportunity to discover and begin to use their spiritual gifts. Everyone would feel more responsibility than before for the life and growth of our own congregation. The celebration would not be our concern at all—that is amply provided for by the staff of the church as a whole.

I feel so strongly about the need for combining the membership group with the fellowship group that I think joining a congregation ought to be a *membership requirement* for an adult joining a church. As a part of the membership class, the adult candidates should be required to become aware of the various congregations, visit the appropriate ones and, by the time they are taken into membership, decide which congregation they want to join. If this were done it would strengthen a church as steel rods strengthen poured concrete.

The Cell

The third part of the formula is the cell. I mentioned before that the congregation is only the beginning of the fellowship circle. It is possible to fellowship with one or two hundred other people, but it is not possible to enter into the deeper kind of interpersonal relationships that are necessary to meet another important set of human needs. The cell, sometimes called a "small group," is a very special relationship. It is so close to a family situation that I like to call it a "kinship circle" to contrast it from the membership circle and the fellowship circle.

I would feel less than honest at this point if I failed to admit that I am not by nature a small group person, nor is my wife. However, I do listen to my pastor who has told me more than once: "You're a fine Christian, but you'll be a much better one if you let God get a hold of you in a small group." I think he's probably right, and I keep trying, but feebly.

I also listen to people like Larry Richards who have a deep personal involvement in spreading the small group movement through churches in America. Here is how he defines the cell: "Eight or twelve believers gathered to minister to each other, to grow in their sensed love and unity, and to encourage one another to full commitment to Christ."[5]

Circles of Concern

Pastor Daniel Baumann of the Whittier Area Baptist Fellowship has utilized the small group dynamic for church growth as well as anyone else I am aware of. His church, a spinoff from another Baptist church, began with 350 members in 1971 and has grown steadily to 820 members in four years. This figures out to a rate of 740% per decade, and this in spite of a facilities problem caused by their sharing a church building with a congregation of another denomination.

Baumann feels that one of the keys to their growth has been what he calls their "Circles of Concern" program. The purpose of this program is "to help us reach out to the other members of the Body of Christ, to assure that no person who comes to our church ever leaves feeling alone or unwanted, but is involved in a meaningful relationship with others who show him love and personal concern."

Each Circle of Concern starts with approximately four couples. Children are also included. The average size is six family units in each circle. They are required to meet at least once a month and also to become involved in some kind of service to the community.

Many meet frequently as well for meals together or for other social events such as a camping trip or a ball game. At the end of each year the circles normally disband and are reorganized with other people. Exceptions to this are allowed if for some reason a particular circle wishes to continue as is.

In 1975 the church counts 32 active Circles of Concern. This means that 192 *families* have developed a level of activity and commitment far above that of the average church member in America. It has contributed to a dynamic growth situation in the Whittier Area Baptist Fellowship, and a similar kind of program will contribute to church growth wherever it is put into practice along with the other major functions.

Remember:

> *Celebration + Congregation + Cell = Church.*

STUDY QUESTIONS

1. Is your church celebration worship service a festival or a funeral? What could be done to stimulate more life in the service?

2. Do you know everyone in your congregation? Do you *have* a congregation? Do you have a number of congregations in your church?

3. What kind of activities characterize a cell? Are you a member of a cell? If so, describe the activity to the rest of the group.

Footnotes

1. Anne Ortlund, *Up With Worship: How To Quit Playing Church* (Glendale, California: G/L Publications, 1975). If anyone wants to know how Ray and Anne Ortlund and Bruce Leafblad do it, he should read this book.
2. Lawrence O. Richards, *A New Face for the Church* (Grand Rapids: Zondervan Publishing House, 1970).
3. Harold L. Fickett, Jr., *Hope for Your Church* (Glendale, California: G/L Publications, 1972), pp. 142-145.
4. Richard A. Myers, *Program Expansion the Key to Church Growth,* privately published brochure, 1970.
5. Richards' book, *A New Face for the Church,* gives many valuable hints about how to develop functioning cells in your church. And Elton Trueblood's *The Company of the Committed* (New York: Harper & Row, Publishers, 1961) is another good book on the subject.

to each his own! why?

The fifth vital sign of a healthy, growing church is that its membership is composed of basically one kind of people.

Even in church, "birds of a feather flock together." And in church growth terminology this is called the "homogeneous unit principle." Its classic expression is found in McGavran's *Understanding Church Growth:* "People like to become Christians without crossing racial, linguistic or class barriers."[1]

The Homogeneous Unit Defined

A "homogeneous unit" is simply a group of people who consider each other to be "our kind of people." They have many areas of mutual interest. They share the same culture. They socialize freely. When they are together they are comfortable and they all feel at home.

Of all the scientific hypotheses developed within the church growth framework, this one as nearly as any approaches a "law." A decade and a half of research dealing with numerous cultures in virtually every corner of the world confirms that the churches most likely to grow are those which bring together in the local fellowship those of a single homogeneous unit.

The Homogeneous Unit Debate

I have spent much time discussing and debating the homogeneous unit principle with Christian leaders of many countries of the world. And without doubt, it is the most controversial of all church growth principles. *Eternity* magazine, for example, recently published a feature article under the title "Where Church Growth Fails the Gospel,"[2] which attacked the homogeneous unit principle with a great deal of verve.

Why the controversy?

Unfortunately, many Americans find the homogeneous unit principle very difficult to accept. Although there are exceptions, Americans seem to have a strong, inherent resistance to approving of churches of just one kind of people. Yet missionaries and Christian leaders from other countries generally accept it almost as a matter of course.

In Burundi, for example, Christian Tutsis have little problem in understanding why Hutus prefer their own kind of local church with their own leadership. Bolivian mestizos tend to give liberty to Bolivian Aymaras to form their kind of church. In Singapore, Malaysian churches and Indian churches and Chinese churches are mutually accepted alongside each other. French Christians do not seem to have difficulty with Gypsies gathering together in Gypsy churches.

In America homogeneous unit churches are also the rule. Even an uninitiated foreigner could readily see that in one city there are Hispanic churches, Oriental churches, WASP churches, European churches and Black churches. A more skillful observer might be able to detect differences between Cuban and Mexican, Japanese and Korean, blue collar and executive, Romanian and Polish, American and West Indian. And even more subtle subdivisions eventually become very important as factors for church growth.

But, while most Americans will admit that homogeneous

churches do exist, many will not go on to say that they *ought* to exist. In other words it poses an ethical problem for them which grew very acute during the civil rights upheavals of the 1960s when the black-white racial struggles seemed to be tearing apart the very fabric of our society.

At a time when racial sensitivities were worn thin, Christian intellectuals developed theologies that led to the conclusion that local churches which mixed homogeneous units were more pleasing to God than those which ministered to only one homogeneous unit. Americans scolded themselves because "eleven o'clock Sunday morning is the most segregated hour in America." The whole thing created some terrible guilt complexes which at least partially account for the reason some oppose the church growth point of view so harshly today.

The debate is intense, the argument long and the issue both crucial and unresolved. Many questions remain yet unanswered, but my own preliminary conclusions as to why some resist the homogeneous unit principle so staunchly can be summed up as follows:

What Happened to Integration?

The residue of guilt produced by the blemish of outright racism and social injustice that has been and is yet perpetrated by WASP Americans on minority cultures hinders an objective consideration of the matter. It also prevents some from catching up with the times. Whereas integration was being suggested as a guiding principle for race relations in the early 1960s, it is no longer regarded as a viable model today.

At the National Conference on Race and Reconciliation held in Atlanta in 1975, for example, none of the black evangelical leaders suggested integration as the wave of the future. They recognize that integration of a minority culture into a dominant culture will inevitably carry with it an undesirable assimilation of black culture into WASP culture. Now that black is regarded as beautiful, black leaders want to preserve black cultural values rather than sacrifice them in a process of social assimilation.

Regretfully, some who formed strong theological ideas on the matter of integration a decade ago are not yet ready to give them up and they tend to surface whenever the homogeneous unit principle is mentioned.

What Happened to the "American Dream?"

The second reason why I think some Americans resist the homogeneous unit principle is somewhat more subtle, but just as powerful. The myth that America is one big melting pot has had a pervasive influence on the American mentality. And it is now difficult for some to accept the fact that the "American dream" has never come true.

All recognize that America is a nation of immigrants, but some also suppose that a social chemistry called "Americanization" begins to operate when immigrants cross the borders and settle down in our land. In time, they are expected to become like "us Americans," usually defined as the white, middle-class kind of American. The dreamer of the American dream hopes that in a generation or two everyone in our country will have forgotten old differences and become like everyone else—all "Americans."

It is disappointing to those who feel guilty about the racist history of American whites and to those who still dream the American dream when they find out that diversity is on the *increase* in America. Instead of becoming more alike, Americans are progressively becoming more different. Immigration patterns indicate that dozens of minor ethnic groups are generating new internal strength around their ethnicity.

Some American Indians, for example, have given up on secularized technology and are now experimenting with a return to a simpler life-style more in harmony with nature. Black women who used to buy hair straighteners and skin lighteners now use a newer line of cosmetics that emphasizes the beauty of their blackness. Chicanos in California and Cubans in Florida are successfully demanding that their children be schooled in Spanish with English being taught only as a second language.

113

Pluralism Is Here to Stay

What this all means is that America is a pluralistic society and probably will be forever. The great lesson that Americans have learned from the turbulent 1960s was that they must come to terms with pluralism. Our attitude ought not be that those different from us would be better off if they were more like us—that is properly labeled "cultural chauvinism." Our attitude, rather, should be that we recognize our cultural differences, while respecting the cultural integrity of Americans different from us. And we should promote laws which will guarantee—much better than our present laws do—liberty and justice for all, not liberty and justice only for those who are most like "us," or who are most "American" according to our dream of what an American ought to be like.

Christians who are not comfortable with cultural pluralism and those who do not understand its full implications will continue to reject the homogeneous unit principle. They usually attack it as a denial of the doctrine of Christian unity and a return to racism.

Racism Is Sin

It should be evident by now, however, that the homogeneous principle is just the opposite of racism. It is based on a high view of culture. It advocates the propriety of churches developing their Christian life-style in ways appropriate to the culture of their members.

The homogeneous principle opposes what some have called the "cultural circumcision" which is inevitable if those of one culture are forced to become Christians in a church of a different culture. It affirms the New Testament principle that Gentiles do not need to give up Gentile culture and adopt Hebrew culture in order to be accepted as the people of God.

It must be admitted, of course, that some churches are racist. Some white churches in America, for example, exclude blacks from membership. Some even forbid them from attending services. This is racism, and it must be condemned on biblical grounds.

Racism is sin and God hates it. So should His people. No

church growth person that I know would advocate that a church be racist and exclude others because of their skin color or their foreign accent.

Now, having said this, we need to recognize that it is altogether possible for a church to develop within one homogeneous unit and still not be racist. I think my own church is one example.

Pasadena is a pluralistic community. Our school district contains 43% whites, 43% blacks, and the balance is made up of several other ethnic units. We maintain the racial proportion in all our schools by busing children from one side of town to the other.

About half of my own neighbors are black. Day in and day out, we experience American social pluralism. Not that we have attained any ideal of social justice—we have a long way to go—but we keep trying.

There are many fine Christian people in our community, some blacks, some whites and some from other ethnic groups. For reasons easily understood according to the homogeneous unit principle, while black Christians and white Christians in Pasadena love each other in the Lord and while they consider each other on an equal plane as citizens of the Kingdom of God, when it comes to joining a local church most blacks prefer black churches and most whites prefer white churches.

Why?

Blacks say, "We've got soul."

Whites say, "We maintain dignity."

Lake Avenue Church is one of these dignified white churches. Not only is our homogeneous unit white, but it is more specifically described by David Woodward as "predominately middle and upper middle class white."[3] However, it is not a racist church.

Any Christian at all who agrees with our philosophy of ministry and to whom our theology of worship appeals is free to become a member of Lake Avenue Church with full standing. A recent count found that there were 25 blacks, 15 Asians and 15 Spanish Americans in full membership in the church.

No one has taken a count, but there are also a considerable number of whites from the lower socio-economic levels and a few from the upper social class. Nevertheless, the homogeneous unit is clear and our entire church life-style is geared to meet the basic needs of this unit. This is one reason the church is growing.

Show me a growing church, and I will show you a homogeneous unit. There may be some exceptions to this rule, but I have not found one yet, and—if there are any—they will probably be the kind of exceptions that ultimately prove the rule.

Who Can Reach Archie Bunker?

As I was researching two churches in the Chicago area one summer, I came across a fascinating contrast in homogeneous units. One was First Baptist, Hammond, Indiana, and the other was Circle Church of Chicago. Each church has its defects, of course, but the strengths of each far outweigh their deficiencies. And both are fine examples of contemporary American churches.

I was intrigued, however, to discover that the members in each church who were aware of the other had a very low opinion of each other. Though I doubt they meant it literally, some people in First Baptist Church questioned whether Circle Church members were really saved. And one or two people in Circle Church—certainly not those in leadership positions—were inclined to label Pastor Jack Hyles a heretic!

In my opinion, this very attitude is one of the defects of each of the churches. I don't think it would have occurred if each had been aware of and accepted the homogeneous unit principle. I hate to say it in so many words, because my friends in Circle Church get irritated when I do, but both are clearly homogeneous unit churches.

First Baptist is located in one of the most industrialized areas of America. A substantial part of the population of Hammond, Indiana, is made up of blue collar workers and their families. As I met and talked to members of First Baptist, I found that a large number of them are shift workers who staff the factories and related services of the area.

First Baptist members are used to taking orders and working

hard for a living. They are well dressed, but they have callouses on their hands, and many have dirt under their fingernails. The men wear their hair closely trimmed, and some have crew cuts.

Most of the First Baptist membership carry King James Bibles. And they paste patriotic bumper stickers on their cars. They are clearly a slice of middle America.

As I soaked up the atmosphere of First Baptist, it occurred to me that this is just the kind of church that could minister to Archie Bunker if he were converted. In fact if he ever does get converted, the odds are very high that it will be through the gospel preaching of a church just like this one. What a bus captain Archie would make if he only knew the Lord!

But I doubt if Archie Bunker would be attracted to a church like mine: too many beards and too few patriotic bumper stickers. Besides, Lake Avenue sold its last church bus some years ago.

Circle Church would be even less likely than mine to get an unconverted Archie Bunker to consider the claims of Jesus Christ. All he would need would be one look at the blacks, the miniskirts and maxiskirts, the college-level books on the booktable, the *Post American* for sale in the magazine rack, the dashikis, the long hair and men wearing beards to make him look for the door. Then if he heard the soul choir, the heavy social implications of the sermon—which he would probably interpret as "pinko"—the abstract level of conversation in the corridors and the avant-garde worship format, he would disappear once and for all.

Circle Church is an interesting case study in itself because it is composed of a rather unusual homogeneous unit. Rather than being a unit determined by racial, linguistic or class differences—all of which are fairly evident when they are present, it is determined by psychological factors—which may be invisible to the casual observer.

Why the Principle Works

To this point we have described homogeneous units and given some examples. The question now remains: What makes them work? Why is it that churches made up of only one kind of people grow better than churches that mix different kinds of people?

It is important to keep in mind that the focus here is on evangelism, not Christian nurture. At this place some people get confused and mislocate the issue. They tend to forget that the basic question is: How can we establish an effective base for winning unsaved people to Christ? Instead they get sidetracked and ask: How should Christians show their love and fellowship for other Christians different from themselves? The first question has to do with evangelism, the second with Christian nurture.

If a given church decides to establish a philosophy of ministry around the principle of becoming a public showcase of racial integration, it can be done. After all, Christians are filled with the Spirit of Christ. In Christ there is no difference between Jew and Gentile or black and white. Bringing Christians from diverse cultures into a local fellowship will not be an easy job because it will require a degree of cultural circumcision on both sides, but with sufficient dedication, effort and sacrifice, it can happen. However, when the task is completed, the resulting church will in all probability find itself almost impotent as a base for effective evangelization in the future.

Some churches have actually found this to be the case, and they have theologized their lack of growth away. They feel that they reflect the true model of the Kingdom of God, they call their experiment "radical discipleship" and they are satisfied that God is smiling on their efforts even though they are not winning many to Christ. It might well be that He is.

But too often such churches are scornful of other churches that have developed different philosophies of ministry, particularly those which are composed of a single homogeneous unit. They tend to say that the other church may be growing in quantity, but at the expense of the quality of a biblical gospel. They often accuse the other of dispensing "cheap grace."

The key question posed by the homogeneous unit principle is not how will Christians react to each other, but how will *unbelievers* who know nothing of the Spirit of Christ react to

118

the preaching of the gospel as they themselves perceive it? Church growth believes that evangelism is not completed with mere decisions, but that the decision must be validated by responsible church membership.

There is no such thing as true commitment to Christ without commitment to the body of Christ. Part and parcel of the preaching of the Gospel should be the implication that the person who accepts it also joins a local church. The church must not be something written in fine print or sneaked in afterwards when the new convert is caught off guard.

If this is true, an intelligent unconverted person, considering the claims of Christ will ask either outwardly or inwardly: "If I do this, what am I getting myself into? What kind of a group will I be expected to join?" So he takes a look at the church.

Remember, he is not a Christian. He knows nothing of middle walls of partition, of Jews and Gentiles, of bond and free. It is natural for him to ask himself: *"Are they my kind of people?"*

If the answer is yes, he will be able at least to hear the gospel. But if the answer is no he will not even hear what is being proposed. In other words, Archie Bunker could be expected to hear the gospel from First Baptist, but less from Lake Avenue and even less from Circle Church.

Let's hope that once Archie Bunker became a Christian his bigotry and arrogance and selfishness would be transformed by God's Spirit into respect and humility and generosity. He would be a new creature in Christ. But there is no biblical requirement that I know of that would force him to violate either his own personality or his own family obligations or his own culture. He would still prefer to identify with "my kind of people"—now "Christian people"—and join a church where he could feel at home. If he did so, he would be ever so much more likely to win his friends on the loading dock to Christ.

Judaizing and Gentilizing

The Bible calls those who make changing culture a requirement to become a Christian "Judaizers." In New Testament days, many people thought that the only people whom God would accept as bona fide members of his family were those who were circumcised, who kept the Sabbath and who followed the Mosaic law. Many portions of the New Testament were written in the context of this problem, since the apostle Paul and others saw more clearly than the rest that Gentiles could become Christians and still keep their Gentile culture.

It was as much a scandal to some in those days to think that Christians would continue to eat pork or go uncircumcised, as it is to some today to think that Christians can drink wine or wear beards or vote for George Wallace. So the Judaizers tried to put a stop to it, and wherever Paul went telling Gentiles that they could have churches with their own Gentile life-style if they wanted to, they followed behind and told them that they'd better form Jewish style churches or else. They were ultimately condemned, of course, both in the Council of Jerusalem and in epistles such as Galatians and Ephesians.

An interesting reversal of this phenomenon has surfaced in our day. Within the last three or four years many of those involved in evangelizing the Jews have begun to apply the homogeneous unit principle with a great degree of success. They suddenly realized that the philosophy of what was called the "Hebrew Christian movement" was really a subtle form of modern day gentilizing.

By suggesting that the normal thing for a converted Jew to do is to join a Gentile church, they were asking the Jew to commit cultural suicide. Through the years some did it, but not very many. The agony was so great that some Jewish families even held funerals for their family members whom they perceived as cultural traitors.

A few years ago, a number of workers deeply involved in Jewish evangelism such as Manny Brotman, James Hutchens, Phil Goble and others became very much disturbed with the unfruitfulness of their work through the years. Independently they came to a similar conclusion: The problem might be more *cultural* than *theological.*

120

Is there any way a Jew can believe in Jesus and still be culturally Jewish?

They knew from experience it couldn't be done well in Gentile churches, so they developed what is now called "Messianic Judaism." The biblical model for their Christian community is Jerusalem rather than Antioch, so they don't even call themselves Christians. They prefer to be known as "followers of Jeshua Hamashiac."

They meet in messianic synagogues on Friday night rather than in Christian churches on Sunday. They circumcise their children and keep Kosher kitchens. They love Gentiles, and any Christian Gentile who wants to can join their synagogue—without being circumcised, but they make no mistake about it—their homogeneous unit is thoroughly Jewish.

Messianic Judaism will undoubtedly be a powerful evangelistic innovation. In nearby Encino, California, for example, 80 converted Jews were recently baptized into the new Temple Beth Emmanuel in an 18-month period.[4] This compares to what the largest Hebrew Christian mission usually baptizes in *five years.*

One reflection of the growing strength of the new movement was the change of the name of the 60-year old Hebrew Christian Alliance of America to the Messianic Jewish Alliance in 1975.

Basic Guidelines

What are the guidelines which emerge from the homogeneous unit principle?

Here is the first: *The social, racial, cultural, economic and linguistic composition of the local church should as nearly as possible reflect the corresponding marriage and family patterns of the community in which it exists if it is to maximize its evangelistic potential.*

And the second: *In structures which are designed on a level over and above that of the local church, Christians should demonstrate practical ways and means of modeling their love and concern for those of other homogeneous units in a public way.*

This is to say that the homogeneous unit principle should operate in what we have called previously the membership circle and

121

the fellowship circle if the church expects to grow well. However, it need not operate in what I would like to call the "citizenship circle," referring to citizenship in the Kingdom of God. It is on this level that Christians need to demonstrate that the walls of partition have in fact been destroyed in Jesus Christ, and I am ashamed to say that on the whole we have done poorly. Perhaps one of the reasons for this has been that we have not thoroughly understood the homogeneous unit principle and the levels on which it should and should not operate.

The Multi-Congregational Model

In some highly pluralistic communities such as inner cities, there may be a new and better way to relate the membership circle to the fellowship circle. A creative model seems to be emerging under the leadership of Pastor James Conklin of Temple Baptist Church in Los Angeles. His church, located right on Pershing Square in the heart of the city, is operating on what they call a "multi-congregational model." Within the church are three separate and semi-autonomous congregations: Spanish, Korean and Anglo.

Conklin, a veteran missionary from Thailand, has the oversight of the whole thing, but functions as pastor only of the Anglo congregation. The Spanish and Korean congregations each has its own pastor and lay leadership and congregational life-style. The cultural integrity of each is fully respected by the others. The congregations ordinarily worship separately, but on the first Sunday of each quarter a special celebration takes place called the "Sounds of Heaven." I attended one and found it spectacular. It is a multi-colored, multi-cultural festival of music, rejoicing, baptisms, new members, sharing and prayer. The congregational singing mixes three languages into the same tune and creates an uplifting cacophony of sound that may well reflect something of what heaven will, in fact, be like.

Notice that the way Temple Baptist does this is to create two levels of membership. Three membership circles on one level obey the homogeneous unit principle. The total membership circle on the higher levels blends with what I called previously the citizenship circle and combines homogeneous units. The experiment is new, but it will bear close watching. It has outstanding potential for effective inner-city ministry.

Temple Baptist illustrates how the homogeneous unit principle can be used positively in an inner-city situation. But let's look next at another inner-city situation which illustrates how violating that same principle can have negative results in a similar urban setting.

STUDY QUESTIONS

1. What does the author say about a homogeneous unit? Discuss this as a group.

2. It has been said that America is a melting pot. It has also been said that the pot has not gotten hot enough. What is your feeling about a pluralistic society where people remain "unmeltable"?

3. Why is it that the homogeneous principle works in evangelism? Why the high priority of evangelism? Why is it necessary for a church to know its homogeneous units?

Footnotes

1. Donald McGavran, *Understanding Church Growth* (Grand Rapids: Wm. B. Eerdmans Publishing Company, 1970), p. 198.
2. Rufus Jones, "Where Church Growth Fails the Gospel," *Eternity,* June, 1975.
3. David B. Woodward, *Life Within and Light Without: The Growth of Lake Avenue Congregational Church,* unpublished manuscript, Fuller Theological Seminary, 1975.
4. Phil Goble sets forth the principles in his book *Everything You Need to Grow a Messianic Synagogue* (South Pasadena: William Carey Library, 1974).

the autopsy of a dead church

Come with me into a church morgue. Here is a collection of corpses—churches that have recently died. They died of many different diseases. Some might have been cured if detected in time, some could never have been cured. In many of these cases their loved ones never knew what happened to them. There was no physician available when the symptoms became acute.

The "pathology of church growth," as this field might be called, is still a young science. But those who have begun to concentrate on it are learning more and more about diagnosing illnesses of churches and curing them with greater frequency.

One of the techniques long used by medical science, but not too frequently by churchmen, is that of the autopsy. With some skillful slicing and testing, a dead body can provide much valuable information. Likewise, dead churches can offer clues that may save the lives of many others.

One of the problems with church pathology is that when a

church's health begins to fail, the people who could best detect what is happening tend to abandon the patient. Top flight pastors do not readily accept calls to dying churches. Denominational executives give higher priority to where the action is developing, not where it is decreasing. Religious editors of newspapers and magazines seek out success stories rather than examples of mediocrity or failure.

Ethnikitis: A Serious Disease

So there are many corpses in this church morgue, but only a few of them carried enough data to their death to be helpful to others. One of these which did is Zion Evangelical Free Church of Chicago. It died on August 31, 1969 of ethnikitis.

Not that I ever heard of "ethnikitis" before doing an autopsy on Zion Church, but the most obvious cause of Zion's decease was an ethnic problem. They were victims of metropolitan ethnic migration, otherwise known as a changing neighborhood. I do not yet know the percentage, but it may well be that ethnikitis is the chief killer of churches in the U.S.A. today.

At the present time I am looking at the graphs of eight Baptist churches of Birmingham. In 1963 they had 2,405 in Sunday School. By 1973 the total had dropped to 161. Today all eight are dead— seven of ethnikitis.

In a word, ethnikitis is caused by a failure on the part of church leadership to understand and apply the homogeneous unit principle to their planning in time. This failure will just as certainly cause debilitation and death in a church as a failure of the liver or the kidneys will in the human body.

Thanks to Pastor David Mains of Circle Church in Chicago, Zion left behind a complete medical history. His book, *Full Circle*,[1] may not have been designed as a textbook on church pathology, but the information it contains is highly useful to put together an understanding of what took Zion to the grave.

Circle Church, Chicago

In recent years, Circle Church has gained a considerable measure of national recognition because of its highly nonconventional approach to the typical problems of an inner city church. This has come about largely as a result of the creative leadership of its two principal staff members, David Mains and Clarence Hilliard, who together form perhaps the most outstanding interracial staff in the nation.

Mains, the founder of Circle Church, refuses to be intimidated by such seemingly adverse inner-city conditions as a highly mobile society, great cultural diversities in the downtown area, changing neighborhoods and the prohibitive costs of property. He built the membership of Circle Church around mobile people instead of sedentary people. Frequent farewells become a normal part of church life from the beginning.

A model called "the open church" was developed to accommodate believers of all races. The dress code that emerged was as permissive as possible. A black man who applied for a staff position, for example, made a favorable impression partly because he came to the interview dressed in a dashiki.

Established in 1967, Circle Church grew rapidly from an original 28 to 500 members-and-regular-attenders—as they like to report statistics—in 1970. The number then dropped to around 350 and has plateaued at that level ever since. Approximately 120 of them are full, active members of the church body. One way they express their commitment is through participation in a number of small "modules," which are task-oriented groupings of men and women who combine their spiritual gifts to accomplish a specific goal. The Circle Church story, which, because of the book, is familiar to thousands of Christians all over America, fairly bristles with valuable lessons for church growth, some positive and some negative.

The first positive lesson is a reinforcement of what we have said here about the first vital sign: the pastor has the power. David Mains is a person very uniquely prepared by God with a combination of spiritual gifts, personal transparency and a heart for relating to people in a warm and supportive way. In the midst of the pressures and tensions that are part and parcel of contemporary inner-city life, he is unflappable. At the same time, he is creative and innovative, not intimidated by the risks involved in attempting new things for God. Very few people I know could have combined such qualities necessary for planting and nurturing a church like Circle.

A second plus was the development of the kind of celebration which met the needs of a significant group of people. The 1960s were the icy winter of the church in the U.S.A. Some were saying God was dead. Some were wishing the institutional church would die as well. Many, particularly the younger generation, were unable to relate well to the traditional stained glass and pipe organs and painted-on smiles that they found in many churches.

But what they saw happening in Circle Church turned them on. Here was a vital Christian group praising God in new ways. No two Sunday services were alike. The pastor seemed to be conversing with them, not preaching at them. The musical mixture of soul and country and rock combined with the traditional helped spice up Christian worship much to their delight. Scores of Christians, most of them under thirty, were attracted by the fresh style of Circle Church.

Another excellent move on the part of Circle Church avoided what some have called the "edifice complex." Few new churches can afford urban real estate. Contracting the Teamsters Union Hall provided excellent facilities at a minimum cost. What's wrong with cleaning up the remains of Saturday night's beer party and worshiping God in the same place on Sunday morning? Since Circle Church economized on building expenses, they could use more of their budget on securing a quality staff, which they did.

The development of the module structure is something that churches across the board should take a look at. By helping church members discover their spiritual gifts and then providing various task-oriented groupings through which they can corporately serve Christ, Circle Church is able to accomplish goals that are out of reach even in many much larger churches. It is a healthy form of decentralization as well as a good vehicle for layman's lib. For example, the Urban Module is deeply involved in the significant "Austin Project," designed to move Circle Church members into a depressed area of Chicago, largely black; to identify with the pains and problems of the community and to develop a holistic Christian ministry to youth, elderly and others; to provide counseling, legal aid, health support and higher quality education.

People Blindness: A Serious Handicap

These and many other positive lessons for church growth emerge from the story of Circle Church. However, the principle reason for bringing Circle Church up at all in this chapter is to show how it relates to church pathology. In introducing Zion church, I mentioned the church disease called ethnikitis. Circle Church is suffering from a second kind of malady called "people blindness."

The term "people blindness" was popularized by Ralph Winter in his plenary session address at the International Congress on World Evangelization held in Lausanne, Switzerland in 1974. People blindness is not usually terminal, like ethnikitis, but it is a definite handicap. It blurs perception and to different degrees distorts reality.

People blindness comes from a failure to recognize the homogeneous unit principle of church growth. In its severe forms, it can become cultural chauvinism. In its milder forms it simply results in a low view of cultural integrity. The Circle Church case is, I think, a mild one, but one that was devastating as far as Zion Church was concerned.

The leadership of Circle Church refuses to accept itself as a homogeneous unit, and they get somewhat irritated when I suggest it is. But they are characteristically fair and open about our differences. I have visited Circle many times, I have talked privately to the pastors and the members, I have met with modules, I have been invited to dialogue on the subject with Pastor Clarence Hilliard from the platform on a Sunday morning.

Circle Church leadership believes that what they call the "open church" is the most biblical model of the Kingdom of God on the local church level. They interpret the New Testament passages on the subject to mean that Gentiles and Jews should both meet together in local churches which are neither Jewish nor Gentile, but in which both cultures are respected. I once heard Hilliard interpret the apostle Paul as saying, "The open church is not Gentile assimilation or loss of identity by absorption in an inadequate Jewish culture, but a mutual sharing through the cross of Christ of both Gentiles and Jews in the privileges and responsibilities of citizenship in God's new community in an atmosphere where differences are accepted and appreciated." I cannot fully agree with this interpretation, but I think it is an accurate statement of the position of Circle Church's leadership.

Circle Church leaders feel that because they have developed a multi-racial church they have demonstrated the vulnerability of the homogeneous unit principle. In a recent *Eternity* magazine interview, Mains denied that Circle Church was a homogeneous unit in these words: "Our people differ racially, economically, sexually, politically, culturally, educationally, etc. Learning to love one another has been painful and the process is far from over, but we stand before our world testifying that the forces that would divide us are not as powerful as that which holds us together."

Almost as an aside, let me make one observation that may be pertinent. If Circle Church does turn out to be a mixture of homogeneous units, this might be one reason why it is not growing. The homogeneous unit principle is a vital sign of *growing* churches, not plateaued churches.

Of course, it may well be that, in the value structure of Circle leadership, it is more important to mix diverse people than to grow. It may be that Circle does not want to grow. Mains does speak of their "small church philosophy." And a church that does not want to grow should not be expected to grow.

Circle's Homogeneous Unit

I still argue, however, that Circle Church is a homogeneous unit. And I described the outward characteristics of that unit earlier when I contrasted it to Archie Bunker's kind of people. But only recently was I able to label the homogeneous unit of Circle Church in a satisfactory way. And thanks to a neighbor of Circle Church, Andrew Greeley of the University of Chicago's Center for the Study of American Pluralism, I now have the handle I was searching for.

The title of one of Greeley's recent books articulates an attitude common to those who have people blindness: *Why Can't They Be Like Us?*[2] It is a book on America's *white* ethnic groups, showing how homogeneous units have been formed in America without the distinguishing characteristic of different races. One of his chapters is entitled "Intellectuals as an Ethnic Group." When I read it, I found that he had isolated and described Circle Church's homogeneous unit. Circle Church, I now realize, is basically a church of *intellectuals* of all colors and all cultural backgrounds.

I recently held a lengthy conversation with a young couple who had transferred membership from my own Lake Avenue Congregational Church to Circle Church. We discussed many similarities and contrasts between the two churches.

At one point the woman said, "In Lake the people our age would discuss common things like new recipes and how we were doing in raising our babies. But not in Circle. Almost every conversation deals with abstract concepts, new ideas and philosophical or theological categories."

This comment fits in with Greeley's observation that intellectuals are a group set apart. He argues that it is most helpful in understanding the relationship of intellectuals to the rest of society "if we perceive that the intelligentsia is, in fact, an ethnic group."

Greeley helped me understand why I heard one or two people—not leaders—in Circle Church who wanted to label Jack Hyles a "heretic." Greeley, of course, is not writing about *Christian* intellectuals, but what he says fits fairly well. "The intellectual is quite capable of compassion," he says, "for the poor and the black, especially . . . but he is singularly selective in his compassion and in his willingness to understand sympathetically and defend members of other ethnic groups. He finds it difficult, if not impossible, to experience compassion or sympathy, or even understanding, for the United States of America and particularly for its middle-class and working-class citizens—especially if they are over thirty."[3]

Greeley points out that the usual pejorative label pasted by intellectuals on middle Americans—like members of First Baptist, Hammond—who do not share their degree of guilt over white racism is "fascists." "Heretics," I suppose, is a more religious version of the same feeling. And to turn the tables, the middle Americans in the secular world would likely label the intellectuals as "Commies," and Christians would probably make it "unsaved."

So, if intellectuals are an ethnic unit, they are vulnerable to ethnocentricity, just like the rest of the human race. Intellectuals ought to know better, but they also can be people blind, starting with not recognizing their own homogeneous unit. I may be wrong, but I perceive this to be at the root of two significant limitations connected with the outreach of Circle Church.

The first limitation relates to the evangelistic impotence of Circle Church in effectively evangelizing other important nearby homogeneous units. For example, the members of the Teamsters' Union, whose hall Circle rents, would be highly unlikely to consider the claims of Christ as presented to them by Circle members. Those who commute to Circle Church from Wheaton—once voted an "All-American City"—would find it very difficult to witness to their unsaved neighbors and persuade them to become Christians, if that implied joining a church like Circle.

According to David Mains, one of the advantages presented by renting the Teamsters' Hall was that they would bring an evangelical witness to the ethnic groups living in the immediate vicinity: ghetto blacks, skid row winos, Greeks, Puerto Ricans and Appalachian or poor whites. Whereas Circle might be in some vague sense a "witness," it is highly predictable on the homogeneous unit principle that new converts in any appreciable numbers will not be won from any of those groups into the Circle Church fellowship. The nearby Circle Campus of the University of Illinois provides an entirely different prospect: a large community of Circle Church's "kind of people"—intellectuals. They *can* win them.

131

Circle Church and Zion's Death

The second limitation brings us back to where this chapter began. Circle Church's people blindness caused it to become the immediate cause for the death of Zion Church.

I say "immediate cause" because Zion already had ethnikitis before Circle Church came into the picture. Circle Church helped it die, but Zion probably had a terminal illness in the first place. Maybe, as it turned out, it was something like a mercy killing. Another kind of death might have been even more agonizing.

The Austin area of Chicago was at one time a white, middle-class neighborhood into which sufficient Scandinavians had moved to form an Evangelical Free Church. It had become a larger than average city church, around 350 membership, and was drawing new members from the neighborhood which then contained people of the same homogeneous unit. But the racial upheavals of the 1960s brought rapid social change to Austin. A syndrome of white flight set in and the saints began marching from Zion. Within three or four years, Zion church had dropped from 350 members to 30!

Terminal ethnikitis!

Those who stayed on were hearty saints of God. They were not about to let their church go without a struggle. They were desperate for help and were ready to take almost anything that was offered.

Meanwhile, Circle Church had passed their planned optimum number of 200 and were ready either to plant a new church or use their surplus membership to help some dying city church come back to life. They chose the latter, offered their help to Zion, and the offer was accepted. A contract was drawn up and signed on September 1, 1968, binding both parties to a one-year experiment.

For about a month signs of health began to return to Zion, as they often do to a terminal patient when one more medical apparatus is attached to the body. But then, as Mains writes, "the cold, hard light of reality began to dawn." The patient began to fail rapidly.

The symptoms of mixing homogeneous units began to surface almost as inevitably as if a person with type A blood received a transfusion of type B. The heaviest donor in the church left as soon as he heard that blacks would be welcome. A furor went up when some Circle girls showed up in miniskirts. An entire family left the church in protest when a songleader mounted the platform with long sideburns!

Not only did Zion members turn off to Circle members, but the reverse happened simultaneously. Many felt that Zion represented precisely what they had been liberated from. They couldn't stand the traditional church building, the moral legalism, the "stiff, rigid rows of pews"—as Anne Ortlund would say—the stained glass windows and the off-key organ. One or two visits was enough to convince them that they preferred to be with "our kind of people." They felt at home in Circle, but could not feel at home in Zion.

Once the final deterioration set in, death was inevitable. But the contract had been signed, and those involved doggedly stuck it out until the bitter end. On August 31, 1969, the contract terminated, and so did Zion Evangelical Free Church. The next day the corpse was in the morgue; soon afterwards it was cremated. The empty building burned to the ground a few months later.

What Is the Lesson?

The purpose of a church autopsy is to learn something useful for church growth in the future. David Mains says that the greatest lesson they learned from the Zion experience was "that we cannot expect any place to be a carbon copy of Circle Church." This seems to me, however, to be only the beginning of the total lesson that needs to be learned.

Circle Church can reproduce itself, if it wants to, but *only* within its own homogeneous unit. There are dozens of groups of multi-racial intellectuals in American cities who would welcome a church with the Circle Church philosophy of ministry in their midst. Furthermore, although this homogeneous unit is not ordinarily among those most receptive to the gospel, there are probably

133

thousands of unbelievers who would listen to the claims of Jesus Christ if they saw them backed up by a Christian community like Circle. There is considerable evangelistic potential here.

What we all need to learn from this is that people blindness is a deterrent to effective evangelism. We need to respect the depth of human attachment to cultural values as a part of God's creation. We need to see the Christian implications of human diversity in a positive rather than a negative light.

We need to stop asking, "Why can't they be like us?" We need to realize that American society is a fascinating mosaic of cultures and cultural sub-divisions and that members of each piece of the mosaic need liberty in Christ to develop the kind of a church where they can feel at home, and which will attract their friends to the Lord.

To the degree we accomplish all this, we will increase the potency of our evangelistic efforts, and our churches will be able to grow in a new way.

STUDY QUESTIONS

1. What are the characteristics of a church in a community with ethnikitis? Do you know of any such churches? What can be done to treat this serious church disease?

2. How do you feel about the author's description of Circle Church and its philosophy? Do you agree with his critiques? What is your perspective on his suggestion of a homogeneous unit?

3. How do you feel about the author's conclusion concerning Zion's death? Do you think he has proven his point? What do you think is the lesson to be learned here?

Footnotes

1. David Mains, *Full Circle* (Waco: Word Books, 1971).
2. Andrew Greeley, *Why Can't They Be Like Us?* (New York: Dutton, 1971).
3. Greeley, *Why Can't They Be Like Us?*, p. 126.

decisions
or disciples?

The sixth vital sign of a healthy, growing church is that it is using an evangelistic method that works.

Earlier I listed "ruthlessness in evaluating results" as one of the general characteristics of church growth people. If the goals are clear, if we have agreed that evangelism needs to be geared toward making *disciples,* not just decisions, then the methods are almost up for grabs.

Consecrated Pragmatism: Methods That Work

As I have studied growing churches in America, I have not struck upon any one method that is common to them all, or even to a significant number of them. For some churches a very effective method is bus ministry. Some grow by using house-to-house visitation, and many of them have developed their method around the Kennedy Evangelism Explosion model.

Others have found that a Christian parochial school has been a positive factor in evangelism. Still others have found the best approach is a drive-in church, the *Four Spiritual Laws*, television broadcasts, neighborhood Bible studies—or a combination of these and many other methods.

To catalog the various methods that might work in your church or to evaluate one method against another would have minimal value here. Why? Because the right ingredients for your church's most effective method are as complex as the right ingredients for a pharmaceutical prescription. There is no such thing as a patent medicine that will cure all the ills of man and beast, nor is there any universal method of evangelism that will help a church to grow.

Find a Need and Fill It

As to the basic principle for discovering the proper method, though, I would have a hard time improving on Robert Schuller's maxim: *The secret of success is to find a need and fill it.* The methods used in growing churches, diverse as they might be, have all done this. They have offered something that will meet the needs of the kind of people they are ministering to.

At this point again the homogeneous unit principle is helpful. Every different homogeneous unit has a different set of needs. You will have a difficult time detecting people's needs if you do not know their homogeneous unit. Worse yet, if you don't, you might find yourself offering people solutions to problems they don't even have.

The End Justifies the Means

When we imply that evangelistic methods are up for grabs, we are unashamedly recommending a fiercely pragmatic approach to evangelism. It is a common mistake to associate pragmatism with lack of spirituality. Some are rightly afraid that pragmatism can degenerate to the point that ungodly methods are used, and this is not at all what church growth people advocate. The Bible does not allow us to sin that grace may abound or to use means that God has prohibited in order to accomplish ends He has recommended.

136

Pragmatism - Practicality
opinionated - conceited

But, with this proviso, we ought to see clearly that the end *does* justify the means. What else possibly could justify the means? If the method I am using accomplishes the goal I am aiming at, it is for that reason a good method. If, on the other hand, my method is not accomplishing the goal, how can I be justified in continuing to use it?

Precisely at this point some evangelistic methods that have been used for years, even decades, need to be reevaluated. I fear that many have fallen into the trap of developing such outstanding programs with such well-oiled machinery, involving such substantial investments of time and money, that the program itself has become the end. The results, if evaluated at all, are evaluated very timidly.

A biblical proverb addresses this problem directly: "It is pleasant to see plans develop. That is why fools refuse to give them up even when they are wrong" (Prov. 13:19, *TLB*). When are plans wrong? Obviously, when they are not accomplishing the intended objective.

Our intended objective in evangelism and church growth is, we reaffirm, to make disciples. Bringing a person to a decision to accept Christ and to counsel and pray with that person is important as one of the means toward making a disciple. But if the person does not eventually make a commitment to the body of Christ—usually validated by baptism and church membership, there is little to suppose that a disciple has been made.

If all a particular evangelistic method has been doing is to register decisions, it is hard to justify continuing it. Why? Because only accomplishing the *end*—making disciples—can justify the means.

Three Streams of Evangelism

I would like to bring this analysis into contemporary focus by running briefly through the recent history of professional evangelism. As I perceive it, three basic streams of evangelism have been prominent over the past 25 years, with a new stream appearing each decade.

Crusade Evangelism

Crusade evangelism was characteristic of the 1950s and, of course, it continues today. It began to gain prominence with Billy Graham's Los Angeles crusade in 1949. The Billy Graham Evangelistic Association was formed in 1950 and, for at least a decade, holding a city-wide crusade was almost universally considered the most effective evangelistic method.

The crusade involved organizing a local committee of Christian leadership in a given city, enlisting the cooperation of as many churches as possible, encouraging broad prayer support, training large united choirs and counseling teams, contracting a stadium or some other public meeting place, advertising the crusade as widely as possible and then inviting the evangelist and his team in for a given number of days. When the evangelist is through, the task of follow-up was then undertaken by the pastors of the local churches that had cooperated.

Crusade evangelism was criticized by the extreme right and the extreme left for different reasons, but mainline evangelicals fairly well accepted it as a good evangelistic method. Very little was done in an attempt to evaluate the method against the results. One of the reasons for this was that during the 1950s evangelicals were self-consciously attempting to carve a more prominent niche for themselves in American religious life, and the one evangelical who had attained the highest status as a religious leader in America also happened to be the evangelist, Billy Graham. Consequently, few evangelicals in America were in the mood to apply fierce pragmatism to crusade evangelism in the 1950s.

But one person outside America was not so timid. He was Kenneth Strachan of the Latin America Mission, whose father, Harry Strachan, was the most prominent crusade evangelist in Latin America for some time. As Strachan took a long look at crusade evangelism, he began to raise questions about what I now call the "follow-up gap." This is the difference between the number of people who register decisions and the number of those who can finally be counted as disciples. In other words, Strachan noticed that in too many cases there was a great deal of evangelistic zeal and activity, but little church growth as a result.

Saturation Evangelism

Strachan set about correcting the method. In his opinion the basic fault of crusade evangelism was too much dependence on the outside evangelist and too little dependence on the people of the local churches. His answer was the program of total mobilization described earlier.

Strachan knew that the people could not be mobilized without first mobilizing the pastors, and it soon became evident that more time was needed than for the typical crusade. He developed a year-long nationwide program and called it "Evangelism In Depth." This concept quickly rose to prominence in evangelical circles, particularly outside of the U.S.A. Throughout the 1960s it became known as "saturation evangelism" and was a very widely accepted method. It came to America in 1973 under the program of Key 73.

Toward the end of the decade, a few researchers began asking the kind of question about Evangelism in Depth that Strachan—by this time with the Lord—had asked about crusade evangelism. With all the additional time, effort, prayer and money being invested in this evangelistic method, had it really solved the problem of the follow-up gap?

As the results of rather extensive research were compiled over a period of time, it was found that the follow-up gap was still there. I know of no case in which the rates of church growth were increased as a result of this evangelistic method. It had many other positive effects on Christian people, but it did not pass the test of fierce pragmatism as far as evangelism was concerned.

Body Evangelism

A new effort is now being made in the 1970s to solve the nagging problem of the follow-up gap. It has its roots in the church growth movement and the principles it uses are based on church growth philosophy. The chief advocate of what is being called "body evangelism" is Vergil Gerber of the Evangelical

139

Missions Information Service.[1] From his Wheaton base, Gerber has moved into country after country holding church growth workshops and sharing the concept of body evangelism.

The major innovation of body evangelism is not that it proposes a method that might be substituted for crusade evangelism or saturation evangelism, but that it helps clarify the goal against which any method must be ruthlessly evaluated. The goal is church growth, and students of body evangelism are taught that if a particular method does not contribute to church growth it should be discarded as quickly as possible.

The principles of body evangelism were tested in a controlled two-year experiment among over 40 churches in Venezuela, in which I had the privilege of participating. The decadal growth rate of the churches increased from 60% to 250% over those two years. No guarantee is being made for such dramatic rises in rates of church growth, of course, but as the body evangelism mentality grips missionaries and pastors and evangelists, old methods are being called into question when they do not help churches to grow. An attitude of fierce pragmatism is growing worldwide.

This kind of pragmatism is also *consecrated* pragmatism. It is a biblical attitude. For one thing, it measures evangelistic methods against biblical goals, namely the Great Commission imperative to make disciples of all nations (see Matt. 28:19). For another it takes seriously the notion of shaking the dust off the feet, if results are not forthcoming under certain circumstances (see Matt. 10:14).

It incorporates the attitude of the owner of the barren fig tree when he found that the tree should have been bearing fruit, but was not. "Cut it down," he said. "Why cumbereth it the ground?" (see Luke 13:7, *KJV*). It avoids the foolishness suggested by Proverbs 13:19 when a person can delight in the development of a program, even when it is wrong.

An Autopsy of Key 73

It is generally conceded that America's last great attempt at

140

a nationwide program of evangelism, Key 73, did not live up to expectations. Perhaps another autopsy is in order.

Why did such a promising evangelistic method fizzle?

I have read several post-mortems on Key 73, but none has completely satisfied me. Some have avoided the ticklish question of what went wrong and dealt with what went *right*. It is generally recognized that three things in particular went right with Key 73:

1. Scripture portions were distributed in unpredecented numbers.

2. Home Bible study and prayer groups for Christians multiplied and strengthened the faith of many.

3. New levels of cooperation among Christians were reached.

The Key 73 program touched upwards of 100,000 American congregations, but without any noticeable change in patterns of growth across the board. I was fearful of this and beforehand I pled for the introduction of Gerber manual-types of measuring instruments so that the evangelistic effectiveness of Key 73 could be accurately assessed in the years to come.

I said, "It would be a shame to 'spend many long hours in prayer, interaction, study and research in trying to sort out strategy, materials, methods, and suggestions which we feel can be most effectively used in a great evangelistic thrust for our nation,' as the *Key 73 Resource Book* suggests, and when it is all over, not be able to look back and accurately report whether the effort was a success or failure."[2] And just because no such feedback mechanism was developed, it is not easy now to put a finger on precisely what went wrong with Key 73.

I have spent a good bit of time on the Key 73 autopsy and have concluded that there was a two-fold problem:

The first had to do with *the basic concept of evangelism.* Evangelism was interpreted as proclamation of the gospel rather than as persuading people to become followers of Jesus Christ and responsible members of local churches.[3]

The second basic problem with Key 73, however, relates more directly to the theme of this chapter: *the methods of evangelism.*

141

Hyper-Cooperativism

If, as a result of the autopsy on Key 73, I were to add a third disease to ethnikitis and people blindness, I would call it "hyper-cooperativism." While some cooperation may be good as a method to accomplish certain Christian goals, if it is overdone it can kill evangelistic efforts such as Key 73. In the same way, I believe, too much cooperation was one of the debilitating elements of Evangelism in Depth, and further research tends to reinforce my earlier observation.

The point is controversial, so much so, in fact, that a reviewer friend of mine believed I wrote with tongue in cheek when I suggested in *Frontiers in Missionary Strategy* that Evangelism in Depth went overboard on its principle of "visible unity of the body of Christ." The verse, "That they all may be one . . . that the world may believe that thou has sent me" (John 17:21, *KJV*), has been made to mean too much if it is taken as a contemporary guideline for evangelistic methods.

The danger is that such an interpretation can lead to a false hypothesis, namely that the more cooperation Christians attain, the more effective will be their evangelistic efforts. Those who accept this hypothesis often tend to confuse priorities. Evangelism slips, sometimes unnoticed, from the top of the priority list and cooperation takes its place.

In the whole development of the Key 73 idea, for example, the generating influence was an editorial in *Christianity Today* (June 9, 1967), entitled "Somehow, Let's Get Together." The text mentioned the "debilitating restraints of conciliar ecumenism" and lamented the "fragmented fringes of independency," suggesting that evangelicals take the middle road and fulfill their longing for "dramatic new dimensions of fellowship across denominational lines." The central thrust of this long and tightly-argued editorial was cooperation. Evangelism was mentioned two or three times, but only in passing.

Response to the editorial was very positive. Evangelicals said in a loud voice that they did want to cooperate with one another. But how? After a few consultations, it became evident that one of the major areas where cooperation could most likely succeed was that of evangelism.

Key 73 was then adopted as a program which could serve as an instrument for evangelicals "somehow getting together." So without anyone's intending it at all, evangelism was used as a means to the end of cooperation. The effort was referred to as *cooperation for evangelism,* but deep down it was more realistically *evangelism for cooperation.*

What a mistake! The liberal magazine, *Christian Century,* saw it clearly when it commented in early 1974, "Although Key 73 was labeled an evangelistic effort, its uniqueness lay in its *ecumenical character.*"

Blurring the Focus on the Local Church

One of the major problems with cooperation as an evangelistic method is that it tends to remove the central focus from the local church. *If effective evangelism happens it has to begin and end with the local church* and all that is involved in large cooperative efforts can be distracting.

As I look across America and see growing churches, all of which have developed successful evangelistic methods of one kind or another, I do not know of many which attribute their evangelistic success to cooperation with other local churches. Each one realizes that there is no way that one system of evangelism can meet needs across the board any more than there is a patent medicine that will cure all ills. The more evangelistic methods are tailor-made for each local church, the more likely they are to contribute to local church growth.

I recall working with Pastor Albert Runge of the North Avenue Alliance Church of Burlington, Vermont, on an analysis of his church growth a couple of years ago. His church was then growing at a rate of 644% per decade and had planted a daughter church some years previously. As he studied the fluctuations in annual growth rates, he noticed that the rate for one year was far and above that of the years just before and just after. After a few minutes of reflection, light came to his eyes. "That was the only year," he exclaimed, "that we decided not to go in with the other churches on a city-wide evangelistic program, but to have our own local church evangelistic program!"

Beyond Cooperation

The point I want to make is not that cooperation is a bad thing or that it is wrong for churches to cooperate. But if the kind of cooperation we have assumed to be a help to evangelism over the past few years actually turns out to be a hindrance, consecrated pragmatism says get rid of it and try something that will in fact bring people to Christ and into responsible church membership. It could well be that we have yet to discover new ways of cooperation that will help make evangelism more effective. But if we sanctify the past forms and place them on a pedestal beyond the range of criticism, we will not even begin to look for the new forms.

Another one of our larger evangelistic organizations recently approached me indirectly and asked for suggestions as to how the evangelistic impact of a fine new Christian film could be made more effective in cities across the nation. They had already worked out a system of getting decisions registered on cards. How could more of these decisions become disciples?

I'm afraid my answer was slightly too radical for them, since I suggested that they might need less, rather than more, cooperation from local churches. It occurred to me that in the average city there are many churches that, even if they received a stack of valid blue chip decision cards from people who had been born again and who were part of their same homogeneous unit, they would not be qualified to attract these people into membership. They are static churches and exhibit all the negative characteristics of stagnation. A new believer would need only one exposure to the dull atmosphere, the puny attendance, the boring worship service, the gloom on the faces of many of the members and the negative thinking that often comes through to decide that he wants no part of that kind of a church.

There are usually other churches in the same city, however,

144

that even before the film comes, are well prepared to absorb new believers. How could they tell the difference?

I suggested that they restrict the churches which are allowed to cooperate with them and receive decision cards to those which can demonstrate an annual growth rate of 5% or more. This figures to a decadal rate of 63%. Most churches at that level are in better shape to minister to new believers than those growing at a lesser rate. That move in itself would narrow the follow-up gap.

Another way to do it might be to promote competition rather than cooperation. I wonder what would happen if the whole system were set up and publicized so that copies of each decision card were given to several churches at once. Then they could rush the person who made the decision like fraternities rush freshmen on college campuses. May the best church win! If nothing else, it would make the new believer feel he was wanted, and give him more than one option as to where he wanted to make a long term commitment.

I have no idea whether the above suggestions are workable methods. What I do know, however, is that they can't be much *worse* than methods used previously in city-wide evangelistic efforts. I am simply illustrating in a relevant way the kind of mentality that is necessary for optimum church growth. For, whatever the cost, we must be prepared to discard old methods that have not worked and introduce new ones that do work if we are serious about church growth.

STUDY QUESTIONS

1. How would you go about discovering the best method of evangelism in your community? Name several ways and discuss it as a group.

2. What's your reaction to the contrasting of body evangelism and crusade evangelism? Do you feel that your church could be effective in body evangelism? If so, where would you start?

3. Has your church set a goal for evangelism this year? What is it? If not, why not? Is that goal persuasion centered? If not, why not?

Footnotes

1. Virgil Gerber's highly influential manual, *God's Way to Keep a Church Going and Growing* (Glendale, California: G/L Publications and South Pasadena: William Carey Library, 1973), summarizes many of the principles of body evangelism and provides a handy workbook section so they can be applied to any local church. The book is a best seller in English and is being published in forty other languages around the world.
2. *Christianity Today,* January 19, 1973.
3. A full explanation of this important, but rather technical point, is developed in some detail in my book *Frontiers in Missionary Strategy* (Chicago: Moody Press, 1971), pp. 124-134.

are your priorities in order?

The seventh—and last—vital sign common to healthy, growing churches in America is that they have their priorities straight. Such churches have come to realize, either intuitively or analytically, that the most important function their church has in its community is a *religious* function.

What Are Churches For?

Throughout his book, *Why Conservative Churches Are Growing,* Dean Kelley deals with the matter of priorities.[1] What are churches for? What do people in an average American community expect of a church?

Dean Kelley is a sociologist of religion who works, not for conservative churches, but for the National Council of Churches in New York City, comes through loud and clear. In his opinion, the one indispensable function of the church in America is to explain the meaning of life to people in ultimate terms.

147

What Do People Need?

People are hungry for many things. They are hungry for food, for employment, for more adequate housing, for recreation, for financial security, for good health, for more stable marriages, for companionship and for God. Churches can, and do, help meet all these needs to one extent or another. In all of them but one, however, they are aided and supplemented by other social institutions, some government and some private.

The one acute human need that churches and *only* churches can meet is the desire to relate to the ultimate, to know God personally. In plainer biblical language, churches are places where people can be saved. No other social institution can match that claim.

Churches may choose to major in functions other than bringing people to God. They may desire to become model agencies for social reform, for example. Certainly there is nothing at all wrong with social reform as a legitimate Christian activity. But to the degree churches allow it to become the top priority in their church life, they will find that their potential for growth is reduced.

The pastors of the growing churches I have studied knew this fact of life before Dean Kelley wrote his book. Their top priority has been right along to bring lost men and women, alienated from God by sin, into reconciliation to Him through the blood of Christ. Gospel preaching is the most important thing they do. They are not indifferent to the social ills around them, but most of them have long since come to realize that God did not call them to be political activists or social engineers. God called them to be pastors, shepherds of the flock, and they cannot be faulted for giving their pastoral function top priority.

Typically, pastors of growing churches avoid even mentioning the burning social issues of the day in their pulpits. In one of his lectures, Robert Schuller straightforwardly advises pastors not to be controversial from the pulpit. "In controversy," he says, "you may relieve your frustration, and you will certainly earn enough opposition to boast that you are 'being persecuted for righteousness sake.'" He warns, however, that in almost every

148

instance to engage in controversy will do the cause more harm than good.

This same attitude is roundly condemned by many other pastors today, particularly by those who received their seminary training during the 1960s, the heyday of social activism. Many of them have since modified their attitudes to keep up with the times, but many would still rather lead their church into a posture of what they consider to be social relevance, even if they know ahead of time that their church may decline in numbers if they do so. I was recently in a social action-oriented church where the pastor believed so strongly in preaching on social issues that he caricatured others as promoting "home-on-the-range churches" where "never is heard a discouraging word"!

Predictably, his church is not growing, but this is of little concern to him. What he and many others like him have yet to learn is precisely the major finding of Dean Kelley's research: Churches that concentrate on developing a philosophy of ministry around social activism tend, in the long run, to *lose* social strength. This is ironic, since the intentions of socially-oriented pastors are just the opposite: They would love to change the world. But the frustration level in churches like this is frequently high because it usually doesn't turn out that way. Dean Kelley himself says that he would be delighted if his thesis were disproved, but "it will take more than insistence to disprove it." He says that he has searched for 20 years for just one case which would disprove the theory, but has not yet found it.

What About Liberal Churches?

In his book, Kelley explains sociologically why liberal churches are not growing. He points out that all social organizations offer what could be likened to a menu for the general public. It contains a presentation of the offerings intended to attract people to join that particular organization.

Many liberal churches will offer art or music appreciation, instruction in women's liberation, guidelines as to which political causes to support at a given time, dialogues with important community leaders and other such activities. But if this is the menu the church offers, few people are interested.

Why? Because the competition in these areas is too keen. Ours is a free society where people can choose what they will join and what they will not. And since almost anyone can find equal or better opportunities for political, social or academic involvement in secular organizations than most liberal churches can deliver, they reject the menu and choose not to join.

"Conservative churches, on the other hand," Kelley goes on to say, "offer an incentive (or commodity?) that is not widely available—salvation—and offer it persistently."

And What About Some Conservatives?

Admittedly, not all conservative churches are growing either. Kelley, and everyone else, knows this. We have all seen or belonged to rock-ribbed conservative churches which show all the signs of strictness and which persistently offer salvation, but which are dead on the vine.

But all this only reminds us that church growth is a complex matter. If a church declares that saving souls is its top priority, but violates a half-dozen other church growth principles, it cannot expect to grow. So a better title for Kelley's book might have been *Why Liberal Churches Are Not Growing*, because there are precious few examples of churches which violate this particular church growth principle of first things first and which continue to grow.

Can Growing Churches Serve, Too?

Contrary to what some would suspect—or even hope, the measurable social good that is being accomplished by growing, conservative churches probably far exceeds that of their liberal counterparts generally. Since liberal churches rather consistently lose social strength, their practical contribution to social change often becomes tokenism. A manifesto here, a contribution to a labor union there, some signatures on a petition, a headline or two, a poor family helped back on its feet—all commendable activities—but year after

150

year there is little that really makes much difference. If the number of members continues to decline, the resources will also decline, and even less will be possible than before.

When a church is growing, however, and when large numbers of people are excited about giving themselves and their resources to serving God in all ways, a great deal can be done. Take, for example, the First Baptist Church of Hammond, Indiana, a church which is showing most of the vital signs of a growing church. Over the past ten years the growth in Sunday School attendance—the one statistic that seems most significant to Pastor Jack Hyles—has maintained a decadal rate of over 400%. The average throughout 1974 was 13,505, and on one Sunday early in 1975 the attendance in Sunday School topped 30,000, a national record. A total of 32,000 names are on the church roll, and Hyles estimates that 20,000 different people pass through the church for some kind of ministry every week.

There is no question about priorities at First Baptist. Even a casual visitor would immediately learn that the church feels its primary responsibility is soul-winning. Hyles says, "The soul-winning fundamental churches are the only hope of America. I want to build a New Testament church that can be reproduced all over America to help save our nation."

One could easily conclude, and many do, that this kind of language reflects an overly narrow view of the whole man. Hyles has frequently been accused of treating people as if they didn't have social as well as spiritual needs. He has heard it many times, and he has this to say: "Our primary aim is to win souls; any social work we do is secondary." Then he continues, "our church does more social work secondarily than most liberal churches do primarily."

It would be an interesting study to compare the social ministry of First Baptist to the other churches in Hammond, liberal or conservative. His claim might well prove out.

Helping the Handicapped

Seeking out and ministering to the handicapped is one of the ways the people of First Baptist show their compassion for some of the less fortunate people of society. By identifying with the deaf, the blind and the educable slow, they are relating to the outcasts of American society in a way reminiscent of how Jesus related to the outcasts of His day.

For example, there are 17 million deaf in the United States today. Theirs is a lonely world. They feel that those who hear misunderstand, ridicule, pity and even ignore them. Their fellowship on any meaningful level is restricted to other deaf with whom they can communicate in sign language. Very few churches have developed the professional skills, the attractive program or the staff to meet their needs in any significant way.

At the last count I have, 250 deaf were enrolled in the deaf program of First Baptist in 14 different classes. One of the challenges kept before the people of the church who can hear is to participate in Christian service by becoming a trained deaf interpreter. Here is the challenge: "As an interpreter you will, no doubt, interpret in the doctor's office, lawyer's office, courtroom, and hospital; for funerals and weddings; in finding employment for them, etc. It may become hectic but it is never dull. May the Lord give you wisdom as you labor for Him with the 'overlooked' people in your home town and area."[2]

Educating Educable Slows

Few of the ghetto dwellers in the darkest inner cities of our country are quite as severely alienated by society as are the mentally retarded. And few people of any color have taken up their cause with zeal. Since they are incapable of writing articles or marching through streets or burning buildings, they have not been able to launch a liberation movement for themselves like many of our other minorities have. They number six million, so they constitute a considerable segment of American population.

The educable slows are another group of needy and oppressed people that First Baptist has compassionately related to. Under the supervision of well-trained personnel, 450 educable slows receive the love, care and fellowship of persons who give themselves in the spirit of Christ, expecting no reward whatsoever except from their Lord. Ten closely graded Sunday School classes have been designed and staffed to help meet their needs.

And there is more! Now that the deaf and mentally retarded programs are moving in First Baptist, a similar one has been started for the blind. The church also distributes numerous free hot meals to the poor each week, collects and distributes clothes and provides food baskets and money to families in need.

A full-time staff member is assigned to shut-ins and handicapped. The church operates the Hammond Rescue Mission to minister to the destitute of the city. Plans are on the drawing board for a senior citizen housing complex and an orphanage.

Illustrations do not have to be multiplied to further substantiate the point that growing churches put their spiritual responsibility first and, as a result, many of them are able to exercise their physical and social responsibilities in a greatly expanded and highly relevant way.

Three Biblical Priorities

No one I know has worked out the biblical principles for setting priorities better than Pastor Raymond Ortlund.[3] With few exceptions, every member of his Lake Avenue Church knows that the three principles are: (1) commitment to Christ, (2) commitment to the body of Christ and (3) commitment to the work of Christ in the world. They are used so frequently around the church that to say "Priority One" or "Priority Two" is as common and mutually understood as "choir practice" or "missionary committee."

The promotional brochure given out to first-time visitors lets them know that these priorities are "in cement." In other words, even before joining a membership class, people are informed as to what the church is about. No surprises after the fact!

Priority One

Pastor Ortlund interprets Matthew 6:33 (*KJV*) literally: "Seek ye *first* the kingdom of God, and his righteousness; and all these things shall be added unto you." There is nothing that can substitute for relating to God and to Jesus Christ as Lord as the *first* step in the Christian life. If people have not become new creatures in Christ, if they are not in touch with the Holy Spirit, if their life-style is not a constant walk with God, they are not prepared to fulfill Priority Two or Priority Three. Christians must live from the center out, and the center is God.

Priority Two

The second priority is second only in order, not importance. These are not three *options* from which Christians may pick and choose. Christian life is incomplete without all three operating in harmony.

For these priorities to make a difference in your life, however, it is necessary for you to understand their precise order. There is no way to start with Priority Two or Priority Three and work back. Priority One is first, but if it does not lead through decisively to Priorities Two and Three, it can and will go sour.

Priority Two is stated like this: "We are committed to each other in Christ. We are called the body of Christ. So we are connected and made to be dependent on each other in His body. That means we must love and care for each other."

Ortlund and his people believe that there is something phony and unbiblical about people who claim a relationship to God, but who do not commit their lives in love to other Christian people. The Bible has too much to say about Christians being members of a body to give much credibility to the person who says, "My church is out there beside a babbling brook on the hillside."

Unless Christian people put it all together and model love, concern, generosity and sacrifice among themselves, they will not be well prepared to share with those who are not yet Christians. God's word tells us that as we have opportunity we should do good to all people, but "especially unto them who are of the household of faith" (Gal. 6:10, *KJV*). "By this shall all men know that ye are my disciples," Jesus said, "if ye have love one to another" (John 13:35, *KJV*). Loving one another is Priority Two.

154

Priority Three

Priority Three is the work of Christ in the world. Not only does the Bible instruct Christians as to how they should relate to one another, but it also gives them some commands as to how they should relate to those who are not yet Christians.

These commands are clustered around two major focal points which are called different things by different people. Jack Hyles calls them soul-winning and social work. Theologians refer to them by the Greek words, *kerygma* and *diakonia.*

My colleague, Arthur Glasser, has popularized the terms, evangelistic mandate and cultural mandate. Others have described them as the vertical dimension and the horizontal dimension, or redemption and humanization.

Evangelism and Social Involvement

Not that the words matter much, but I like to describe these two focal points as evangelism and social involvement. Both are part of Priority Three. Both need to be done if the Christian is to model his commitment to the work of Christ in the world.

As far as I can tell, the leadership of every growing church in America would affirm their agreement with this. But they also know something more than this. They know that within Priority Three is a set of subpriorities. They consistently give evangelism the priority over social involvement, even though they attempt to do both.

To go back to Lake Avenue Church for a moment, here is how Priority Three is explained in the brochure given to visitors: "We are committed to the work of Christ. We want this world to know the Savior who died for all. It makes no difference what color or age or social status or nation.

"We crave to tell everyone that 'God so loved the world that he gave his only begotten son!' God thinks all men are worth that! That's good news! That's the Gospel!"

Notice that the stress is on evangelism. Nothing appears in this context about social involvement. If what Dean Kelley teaches

155

us is valid, this is exactly what a church brochure designed for the general public should stress.

People expect the church to say something important to them about the ultimate meaning of life. Christians know that this involves relating to God through Jesus Christ, and call it evangelism.

Prioritization of Evangelism

I must admit at this point that there is no general agreement among evangelicals—to say nothing about liberals—that evangelism should take priority over social involvement. In fact, this was one of the most hotly debated issues at the 1974 International Congress on World Evangelization in Lausanne, Switzerland, and it remains a point of contention on the Continuation Committee of which I happen to be a member. A very good friend of mine, whose evangelical credentials are above reproach, refused to sign the *Lausanne Covenant* because he could not agree with what he called the "prioritization of evangelism."

This is what the *Lausanne Covenant* says about Priority Three: "We affirm that Christ sends his redeemed people into the world as the Father sent him, and that this calls for a similar deep and costly penetration of the world. We need to break out of our ecclesiastical ghettos and permeate non-Christian society. In the church's mission of sacrificial service *evangelism is primary.* . . ." (Article 6).

I heartily agreed with this section of the Covenant and signed it without reservation. I was delighted that such a prestigious gathering of Christians from around the world affirmed the prioritization of evangelism as a church growth principle. Nothing is more important for a church that wants to grow than to make as the first item of its message to those without: "We are ambassadors for Christ, as though God did beseech you by us: we pray you in Christ's stead, be ye reconciled to God" (2 Cor. 5:20, *KJV*).

Evangelism, of course, includes both local evangelism and worldwide missions. Both are essential elements of Priority Three.

Both are inescapable Christian obligations.

Social Involvement Needs Planning

The second subpriority in doing Christ's work in the world is social involvement. Though I have yet to discover a close correlation between social involvement and church growth, on biblical principles alone I firmly believe in it.

Jesus gave us the example. He healed the sick. He touched lepers. He ate with publicans and sinners. He fed the hungry. He cast out demons. He identified with the poor and outcast while at the same time He loved Roman centurions and government tax collectors.

Many Christians make the mistake of thinking that Priority Three will happen spontaneously if they just do well enough on Priorities One and Two. Experience shows that it will not just happen. Effective evangelism usually is a result of planning as well as prayer.

Just because a church is evangelizing well there is no assurance that it will automatically do a good job of social involvement. I cannot agree with the oversimplification that goes: "Saved souls will change society." All too much evidence shows that they often don't.

All too many growing churches have little or no social ministry and unfortunately this turns some people against the whole church growth philosophy. I think such people throw the baby out with the bathwater, but I applaud their efforts to joggle socially uninvolved churches out of their lethargy.

Some growing, evangelical churches are not more socially involved because they don't quite know how to handle the situation. On one hand, they want to do something, but on the other they don't want to do the wrong thing. They are aware of such incidents as the contribution of the United Presbyterian Church to the fund for a fair trial for Angela Davis and the devastating effects of that action on the denomination ever since. They dread the thoughts of making the same mistake.

Evangelicals don't want to fall into the trap that Dean Kelley warns so clearly against. They read books like David Howard's *Student Power and World Evangelization,*[4] learn that a powerful evangelistic organization like the Student Volunteer Movement went under chiefly because social involvement eventually gained priority over evangelism, and they don't want the same thing to happen to their churches.

Social Service vs. Social Action

There is an answer to the evangelism/social involvement dilemma. And the key is found in the distinction between the concepts of *social service* and *social action.*

Social service is designed to relieve immediate needs of people: healing the sick, feeding the hungry, clothing the naked, counseling the emotionally disturbed, finding work for the unemployed and so on.

Social action is something else. It makes the more radical demand to change the structures of society so that the poor and oppressed will get a fairer piece of the social pie, so to speak. Social action ordinarily involves politics of some kind or other. It requires joining parties, forming pressure groups, signing petitions, making public declarations, getting out voters, and even in some cases—as Americans are celebrating in the bicentennial year—outright revolution.

How should churches, as distinguished from Christians as individuals or in groups, relate to social problems according to this classification? I would suggest here a sub-subpriority under social involvement. If churches are going to develop a social ministry (and I think they should), they will do well if they stick to social service and leave social action to other organizations, both secular and Christian.

Though I have not detected a relationship of social involvement to church growth, let me articulate here a related principle, however: *To the degree that socially involved churches become engaged in social action, as distinguished from social service, they can expect church growth to diminish.*

With this principle established, we can outline now the biblical

158

priorities which constitute the seventh vital sign of healthy, growing churches.

Priority One: Commitment to Christ.

Priority Two: Commitment to the body of Christ.

Priority Three: Commitment to the work of Christ in the world.

    Subpriority One: Evangelism.

    Subpriority Two: Social involvement.

        Sub-subpriority One: Social service
        (I hesitate to classify social action as any priority
        for churches—as churches—at all.)

The Seven Vital Signs

Vital signs were developed by medical science to describe what happens inside a healthy human being. Vital signs are also useful to diagnose ill health. Churches also have vital signs—seven of them. A recognition of these signs and their implications leads to an understanding of what happens within healthy, growing churches.

If your church is growing, it will probably score high on most of the seven vital signs. If not, a good place to start the diagnosis would be to measure your church against these signs and try to find where the greatest deviation is taking place.

So here again is a list of the seven vital signs:

1. *A pastor who is a possibility thinker and whose dynamic leadership has been used to catalyze the entire church into action for growth.*

2. *A well-mobilized laity which has discovered, has developed and is using all the spiritual gifts for growth.*

3. *A church big enough to provide the range of services that meet the needs and expectations of its members.*

4. *The proper balance of the dynamic relationship between celebration, congregation and cell.*

5. *A membership drawn primarily from one homogeneous unit.*

6. *Evangelistic methods that have been proved to make disciples.*

7. *Priorities arranged in biblical order.*

159

STUDY QUESTIONS

1. What are the priorities of your church? Are they clearly stated? What are your personal priorities concerning evangelization of the world? What do you feel a church ought to be doing concerning social needs of the community? Do you agree with the author that salvation and the ultimate meaning of life is the highest priority of the church?

2. Do you agree with Jack Hyles' stated priorities that evangelism comes first and social needs must be met secondarily? How is your church relating to these priorities? Are you meeting the needs of people by evangelizing and meeting their social needs?

3. What do you feel about the author's conclusion of social service versus social action? Do you think he has established the priorities? If so, how should this impact your church and its priorities?

Footnotes

1. In some respects, I consider Dean Kelley's book *Why Conservative Churches Are Growing* (New York: Harper & Row, 1972) the most important book for the church growth movement in America.
2. Maxine Jeffries, *Our Ministry to the Handicapped,* mimeographed manual of First Baptist Church, Hammond.
3. In his book *Lord, Make My Life a Miracle* (Glendale, California: G/L Publications, 1974), Raymond Ortlund describes in detail the three biblical principles for setting priorities.
4. David Howard, *Student Power and World Evangelization* (Downers Grove, Illinois: InterVarsity Press, 1970).

god wants your church to grow!

Every so often I get irked at some of my colleagues in the ministry. I don't mind debating the principles of church growth. Whenever I do I learn something more about why some churches grow and why some decline. I don't mind pastors of static or declining churches honestly seeking out reasons why it is happening; in fact I spend a good bit of my time encouraging such self-diagnosis.

But when ministers associated with declining churches come up with *biblical* rationalizations for their lack of growth, I confess I get irked. It is simply biblical and theological nonsense to argue that God is pleased when churches, year after year and generation after generation, lose members.

Is Church Growth the Point?

I refer again to Robert Hudnut's recent book, *Church Growth Is Not the Point.*[1] Here is a whole book attempting to muster theological reasons why God prefers churches to lose members rather than to gain them. He notices that people are leaving the church and says, ". . . it could not be a better sign." In many cases "loss of growth in statistics has meant increase in growth in the Gospel." He rejoices that declining churches get rid of "dead wood" and stay with the "faithful remnant." "Church growth

161

is not the point," he stresses, ". . . faithfulness to our Lord Jesus Christ is."

This is theological slight-of-hand. Notice that Hudnut tries to set church growth *against* the gospel. He even tries to set it *against* faithfulness to Jesus Christ! Those familiar with the New Testament need no detailed answer to such an unbiblical line of reasoning. They know that Jesus commanded church growth, and that Christians who are faithful to Him as Lord will work toward that goal.

The gospel is to be proclaimed to all nations, and the expected response is repentance and faith in Christ. Jesus told us to baptize these people in the name of the Father and the Son and the Holy Ghost (see Matt. 28:19), and if that doesn't mean church growth, I don't know what does.

Heads vs. Hearts?

Even more recently, a pastor in Southern California wrote an article attempting to set church growth against *evangelism*, of all things. He is disturbed because "evangelism has always been connected with church growth." He considers evangelism to be a much bigger term than that. "It certainly must mean more than the recruitment of persons into the life of the church," he argues.

"We count heads," this pastor says. "God counts hearts." He suggests that we have a one-year moratorium on statistics so that we can get down to the business of evangelism. He feels that God's strategy might not be to *extend* the Kingdom of God, but rather to *intensify* it.

Two biblical illustrations are given to buttress this rather unusual view of what evangelism might be. The first is of Gideon who reduced an original 32,000 volunteers to a corps of 300 in order to attack the Midianites. The second is of our Lord who, though great crowds were drawn by His preaching, required that His disciples bear a cross, and ended up dying alone.

Gideon? Evangelism? Certainly Gideon was a hero. His tricky strategy which routed and defeated the Midianites was all part of God's plan for the Israel of that day. But to make this wartime

162

episode a model for all to follow makes little sense either for warfare or for evangelism.

For each example of Gideon's battle tactics, the Bible has dozens of examples of Joshua's style which threw as many warriors as possible into the thick of the battle. Throughout history wars have generally been won by large armies. By the same token world evangelism has been best accomplished when, to use another analogy, the Lord of the harvest has thrust out laborers into the harvest field in great numbers.

Jesus and Church Growth

Relating Gideon to evangelism and church growth requires mental gymnastics of which I am not capable. But relating Jesus himself to evangelism and church growth is something else. After all, Jesus came "to seek and to save that which was lost" (Luke 19:10, *KJV*).

Jesus believed in statistics enough to suggest that the good pastor is the one who knows his sheep well enough to notice that out of 100 sheep, 1 was missing. And when one was missing, Jesus' idea of a good shepherd was not to say, "Oh, that was just a weak sheep: the flock will be better off without him." No, that shepherd went out and searched for the lost sheep until he found it and brought it back (see Luke 15:4-6).

The story of the lost sheep is related directly to evangelism. Jesus says that lost persons need to be sought and found and brought into the fold. When that happens, he says, "Joy shall be in heaven over one sinner that repenteth" (Luke 15:7, *KJV*).

Jesus also said, "I will build my church; and the gates of hell shall not prevail against it" (Matt. 16:18, *KJV*). He was all in favor of church growth. When He talked about the Kingdom of God, He talked about a tiny mustard seed which would eventually develop into a great tree (see Matt. 13:31-32). Growth again!

Jesus knew there would be tares among the wheat as the Kingdom of God grew, but He told his followers not to worry very much about the tares; Hudnut would call them "dead wood."

163

"Let them both grow together," He said, "until the final harvest time" (see Matt. 13:30).

I have a hunch that many of those people whom pastors relegate to "dead wood" are in reality good Christian people who are leaving certain churches in America because: (1) they or their families are hurting and need pastoral care they do not find in those churches, or (2) they are live Christians who find little or no opportunity for exercising their spiritual gifts in dull, declining churches.

Some of these people, unfortunately, might drift away from the faith. A large number of them, however, look for another church more adequately geared to meet their spiritual needs.

Sometimes when this change happens and when a number of people leave Church A and join Church B, Church B is accused of "sheep-stealing." In many cases, however, I think it might better be considered "sheep finding." When pastors like those we have been discussing say "good riddance to the dead wood" as men and women leave their churches, those men and women become sheep without a shepherd. And blessings on the shepherd who is willing to seek them and find them and fold them into a loving congregation.

The next step is for Church A to call a moratorium on statistics so that when the year ends the leaders of that church have no idea how many of their sheep might have been lost. This protects shepherds who care little whether the wolves come in and raid the flock since there is no way they can be held accountable without statistics. But I do not see Jesus commending such a pastor, and I do not feel that lack of church growth should be dignified by attributing it to the will of God.

Was Jesus "Success-Oriented?"

But if Jesus' will was church growth, how did He do? What kind of success did He have? Was He "success-oriented" at all?

After all, Jesus did end up on a cross. And His disciples had either abandoned Him or were watching from afar off. What does all this say to the Church Growth Movement?

Notice that the cross was never an end in itself. It was the means toward another end. Jesus died as the Lamb of God who takes away the sins of the world. He was sacrificed to pay the price of human sins, and He was eminently successful in doing so.

Since He died, the blood of Jesus Christ has been sufficient to cleanse us from all sin (see 1 John 1:7). People who repent of their sins and believe in the power of Jesus' blood to forgive their sins are saved. They become "new creatures in Christ" (see 2 Cor. 5:17), and as such they are called "disciples." Disciples are added to the church of Jesus Christ.

In plain language, therefore, one way of looking at the purpose of Jesus' death on the cross is that it provides the means through which church growth can happen. When men and women are saved, churches grow.

So far, so good. But did Jesus *succeed* at this? Did he give us an example of evangelism and church growth to follow?

I have seen some people wring their hands and make excuses for Jesus at this point. "Well," they sometimes say, "Jesus might not have done much, but He promised us that we would do greater things." Some even compare Jesus unfavorably to the superchurch pastors in the world today.

In my opinion, Jesus needs no apology. As an evangelist He was an outstanding success. He was a missionary to unreached peoples. Yet only three years elapsed between the start and the finish of His active ministry.

Jesus began by winning 12 people to Himself. When He finished, the 12 had become a committed group in Jerusalem of no less than 120 disciples, but more probably upwards of 500—as hinted in 1 Corinthians 15:6. Growth from 12 to 120 in 3 years represents a decadal rate of 215,343% or an annual growth rate of 115%! This is astronomical enough without even figuring it on the basis of 500 instead of 120!

Granted, these figures are not too useful in themselves, since everyone knows that when you start with a small number like 12, the rates of growth become enormous. The proof of the pudding comes in whether high rates of growth can be *sustained* after such a propitious beginning.

Growth in the Books of Acts

What happened to the church Jesus planted in Jerusalem? Did the leaders say, "Let's now see if we can do what Gideon did and reduce the 120 to 60 before we start evangelizing?" No, instead they waited and prayed only until the whole 120 were filled with the Holy Spirit and they began to proclaim the gospel with vigor. What happened after that is a matter of record in the book of Acts, which I take much more as an example of God's will for a healthy church than the story of Gideon or the dark moments on Calvary.

And what exactly does the book of Acts (*KJV*) say happened to this little church that Jesus left behind?

Acts 2:41: Then they that gladly received his word were baptized: and the same day there were added unto them about three thousand souls.

This was the day of Pentecost. Peter and the apostles did their jobs as evangelists. The rest of the 120 exercised their spiritual gifts and nurtured the new converts. When people repented and were baptized the church grew by leaps and bounds. Growth was so rapid that it would be next to ridiculous to figure annual or decadal rates on the basis of 120 to 3,120 in one day.

These 3,000 were really disciples. The fact that there was considerable quantity did not seem to reduce the quality. They "continued steadfastly in the apostles' doctrine and fellowship, and in breaking of bread, and in prayers" (Acts 2:42).

Acts 2:47: And the Lord added to the church daily such as should be saved.

Pentecost was no flash in the pan. The Jerusalem church did not make the mistake of saying, "We've finished our evangelism, let's now enter into a period of consolidation." Jesus had taught church growth principles well enough so that they knew they shouldn't separate evangelism and follow-up. While they nurtured new believers and built their faith, they simultaneously kept evangelizing. The result was that new believers joined the church every day.

How many were added this way? Luke doesn't tell us, but would it be far off to postulate another 3,000? If not, that would make 6,000 total. The next passage does give an exact figure:

Acts 4:4: Howbeit many of them which heard the word believed; and the number of the men was about five thousand.

So much was happening by now, that government officials became concerned. Peter and John were put into prison for their bold evangelistic preaching, but not before they had won 5,000 more. And the 5,000 were only men!

How many women might have been saved also? Perhaps another 5,000?

To make a quick total, the minimum number of disciples at this point would be 8,120 and the more probable number 11,000.

Acts 6:7: And the word of God increased; and the number of the disciples multiplied in Jerusalem greatly.

In two of the three passages quoted above, the word "added" was used. But the church had continued to grow so rapidly that *addition* of disciples now became *multiplication*. Possibly the 215,343% decadal rate we calculated previously wasn't too far off after all.

The Jerusalem church had grown so rapidly at this point that precise figures are impossible. But it seems quite clear that by the time Acts 6 and the persecution came along the church had grown from an original 120 to something between 10,000 and— more likely—25,000.

The Great Commission was being fulfilled. The early disciples who knew Jesus personally interpreted faithfulness to Jesus at least in part as actively spreading the good news and planting new churches.

A good start had been made in Jerusalem. But the Commission said, "Ye shall be witnesses unto me both in Jerusalem, and in all Judea, and in Samaria, and unto the uttermost part of the earth" (Acts 1:8, *KJV*). So, from Jerusalem and Judea, they moved out into Samaria!

And then what happened?

Acts 8:12: But when they believed Philip preaching the things concerning the Kingdom of God, and the name of Jesus Christ, they were baptized, both men and women.

Here we find Philip the evangelist—who in all probability had not even been a Christian when Jesus was crucified—chased out of Jerusalem by the persecution and now planting churches in Samaria. He went from village to village and the church grew magnificently among those people traditionally so despised by the Jews.

Acts 9:31: Then had the churches rest throughout all Judea and Galilee and Samaria, and were edified; and walking in the fear of the Lord, and in the comfort of the Holy Ghost, were multiplied.

By this time the gospel had reached Galilee and churches had been planted there. The interesting thing here is that previously Luke had spoken of *people* being first added, then multiplied, but now the movement is spreading so fast that he speaks of *churches* being multiplied.

Acts 9:35: And all that dwelt at Lydda and Sharon saw him, and turned to the Lord.

Something new happened here. Through Peter, a paralyzed man was healed and, as a result, two entire villages decided as groups to follow Christ. The phenomenon of people movements to Christ has since become an important part of church growth philosophy, even though people movements are rather uncommon in the U.S. and Canada today. In other parts of the world, however, multitudes are becoming Christians through people movements similar to those in Lydda and Sharon.

Acts 11:21: And the hand of the Lord was with them: and a great number believed, and turned unto the Lord.

This passage signals the beginning of church growth among the Gentiles. Previously churches were being multiplied among Jews and Samaritans, but here in Antioch the Gentiles began their time of coming to the Lord. The political situation of that day virtually ended the Christian movement among Jews before the first century was over, but what began in Antioch among Gentiles has continued at an accelerated rate ever since.

Acts 16:14: And a certain woman named Lydia, a seller of purple, of the city of Thyatira, which worshipped God, heard us: whose heart the Lord opened.

This passage concerning the church at Philippi is significant because it marks the beginning of church planting in Europe. This new growth resulted as the gospel spread among Gentiles from Antioch through the missionary activities of Paul, Barnabas and others. And since the ancestors of many Americans were Europeans, the church at Philippi will always hold a special place in their experience.

Acts 21:20: And when they heard it, they glorified the Lord, and said unto him, Thou seest, brother, how many thousands of Jews there are which believe, and they are all zealous of the law.

The word translated "thousands" in this passage comes from the Greek word "myriads" which actually means tens of thousands. In other words, toward the close of the ministry of the apostle Paul—who spent most of his time evangelizing and planting new churches among the Gentiles—the number of Jews who had become followers of Jesus could only be estimated in myriads or multiples of ten thousand.

Could the figure have been something around 100,000? Just for curiosity, if it were 100,000 and the period of time since Pentecost were calculated at 30 years, that Jerusalem Church which started with 3,120 on Pentecost sustained a decadal growth rate of 222%, superb in anyone's book. This says nothing about the results of the ministry of Paul, Barnabas and others who concentrated on the Gentiles.

Jesus Was Successful

So, whether one likes to think of Jesus as "success-oriented" or not, His stated goal of making disciples was a tremendous success for at least 30 years after he planted the first church and went to heaven. Any missionary or evangelist I know would like to be able to report success in similar terms. Not only did Jesus die on the cross for church growth and command church growth, but He also set an example for church growth through His ministry.

This should make the followers of Jesus today tremendously optimistic. God's will is clear. The same Holy Spirit who filled the believers and set them preaching the gospel on Pentecost is here and available today. The Christian movement has spread worldwide so that today, with the possible exception of Afghanistan and the Mongolian People's Republic, every nation in the world now has a community of those who claim Jesus Christ as their Lord and Saviour.

By a conservative estimate, 55,000 people become Christians every day. Every week at least 1,400 new Christian churches are planted around the world.

The harvest is out there, in quantities far too great for the available reapers. Here in the United States it is estimated that at least 100 million people have yet to commit their lives to Jesus as Lord. Not all of them are receptive, but tens of millions are. Chances are that within a short driving distance of your own church are thousands and thousands of people who need the Lord and who would become faithful disciples if they heard the gospel in terms they could understand and relate to.

You Can Be Successful, Too

Many people will not become Christians unless and until your church and hundreds of other churches like yours take seriously the command of Christ to make disciples of all nations. You and your church can participate in the harvest. You can win people to Christ and bring them into responsible church membership.

But it will not happen just because you wish it to. Cases of easy, spontaneous evangelism can be found, but the world will not be won by Christians enjoying each other and waiting for it to happen. Discipleship is costly. Effective evangelism is costly. Part of taking up your cross is seeing to it that what you do contributes to others taking up their crosses also.

170

God's work in the world today will not be accomplished by timid, pessimistic people who rationalize away defeat. It will only be done by those who are sold out for God!

Friend, God wants you and the Christians around you turned on for him. One of the things He wants to use you for is to reach out in love to unbelievers in your community and bring them to Jesus. He wants you filled with the Spirit. He wants others to know and love Him. He wants to add daily to your church such as should be saved.

He wants your church to grow!

STUDY QUESTIONS

1. Review again the author's scriptural basis for concluding that the Church must grow. Do you agree that it was Jesus' intent that the Church would grow and that this process would be directly related to the evangelization of the unsaved? What was the significance of Jesus' death on the cross as it relates to church growth?

2. Did you trace the author's teaching through the book of Acts concerning church growth? What did you see in terms of the keeping of numbers? Does the Bible actually indicate a results-orientation in its philosophy of evangelizing? Is the Great Commission fulfilled then only by the winning of new people to Christ and bringing them into a countable relationship in the Church?

3. What did you think about the statement that 55,000 people become Christians every day, and every week at least 1400 new Christian churches are started? How does this news impact your thinking in relationship to church growth and to having new church offspring from your church?

Footnotes

1. Robert Hudnut, *Church Growth Is Not the Point* (New York: Harper and Row, 1975).

index

172

173

175